TABLE OF CONTENTS

INTRODUCTION

The celebration of the 200th year of independence caused us to think about the reasons for our country's greatness. Since that year of celebration, many living history and American history museums have been established which demonstrate to us how our ancestors lived, fought and worked. The more interesting of these museums, it seems to me, are those with a restored kitchen where food is prepared while visitors watch. There we can see how our ancestors ate.

When I started to do volunteer work at a local museum, I became interested in cooking at the original hearth of that house which had been built in 1796. I had no book to tell me the purpose for the different pots and tools which had been placed in the kitchen, nor was there anyone among the volunteers who had experience in hearth cooking.

Already possessing a love for cooking, I struggled along learning the basics of hearth cooking. I was surprised to discover that in my Southern, country background the cooking still retained the main elements of hearth cooking in Early America— long slow cooking, seasoning with salt pork, bacon grease and herbs; and the use of things which we raised, caught, shot, or could easily obtain. Perhaps I received help from the spirit of my great-grandmother who my mother told me had cooked at a fireplace in her kitchen.

When I began to study the cookbooks which were written in early times, I learned a lot about what was cooked, but found that the author had rightfully presumed that the reader already knew how to cook at the hearth. I then saw the need for *At the Hearth*. Later, when I began to teach, my pupils often expressed a desire for me to write a book on hearth cooking. Visitors to the museum asked for a book for preparing my recipes in a modern kitchen. This book is the answer to both requests. In addition to being a helpful guide in preparing classic dishes, it has been written in the hope that reading it will be fun and informative.

Several excellent recipe books have recently been published which contain hearth cooking directions. My book is different from those books in that they contain many old recipes which are not usually attributable to specific period cookbooks. These recipes, or "how-to's," have been passed down in Southern kitchens and by cooks in Baltimore and other parts of Maryland. Many are for dishes which were served in my mother's South Arkansas kitchen, cooked as they were by my pioneer ancestors. Some are for food prepared in middle-class urban homes or small frontier farms and mountain cabins. They are the directions followed by mothers and daughters preparing family meals with little or no outside help. They are recipes for the food which has sustained generations of Americans.

I have learned to love hearth cooking and to enjoy each hour I spend at the hearth. This is in spite of the fact that it is hard, heavy, and sometimes dirty work. I am inspired by the challenges hearth cooking presents: nothing can be taken for granted; you must be constantly vigilant. I find it satisfying that I must strive to be in control.

Hearth cooking has strengthened my interest in history and in all things old. I have a keener desire to visit old houses and to observe their contents. My joy in searching through and collecting old cookbooks has been heightened. I enjoy "meeting" the authors and acquiring a further appreciation as I compare their methods with modern means for attaining the same culinary goals.

I hope that you will enjoy *At the Hearth* and that you will be inspired to prepare some period meals for your family and friends.

Look back—only to see what was cooking!

CONCERNING HEARTH COOKERY

No hearth cooking instructions should be given without first stressing the importance of safety. We know that the statistics for death by fire were grim in the days when fireplaces were the main means for cooking.

When preparing to cook at the open hearth, pay particular attention to your clothing. Natural fabrics such as cotton or linen should be chosen. If the cook is dressed in period clothing, skirts should be hemmed or tucked so that they will not drag across the coals. Do not cook while barefoot—live coals often pop out of the fireplace. Other than authenticity, a good reason for wearing a cap while hearth cooking is that it will protect your hair from the smoke which is usually in the air around the fireplace.

It is advisable to keep a woolen blanket near the fireplace to smother the flames should an accident occur. A bucket of water and large container of baking soda must also be handy. A modern fire extinguisher should also be kept close by, out of sight in period settings.

Be extremely careful in handling pots, lids, and other heavy iron equipment. Remember that iron holds heat for a very long time. Never use a cloth which is damp or wet to lift hot equipment.

The chimney must be checked annually and all soot and grease removed. Unfortunately, many old houses have been destroyed by fire in the chimney.

Of course, before you can cook at the hearth you must have a fire, and for a novice this can be a difficult undertaking.

However, once you have learned the basics, it is a fairly simple process. Either andirons or two large split pieces of firewood should be set on the light layer of ashes in the fireplace to provide the circulation of air. Lay several pieces of kindling, usually pine which is rich in resin, on the andirons or split pieces of firewood. Crumple several sheets of newspaper and put between and on top of the kindling. Next place more kindling on top of the newspapers, grid fashion, leaving plenty of room for air circulation. Now, place larger pieces of hardwood, resting them on the andirons or base pieces. Light the paper and when the fire is blazing nicely put on larger pieces of hardwood, adding additional wood as it is consumed. One can only wonder at the difficulty of lighting a fire before the invention of matches and the abundance of newspapers. The main challenge for a cook who is accustomed to using modern fuel is remembering that wood must be added constantly to provide heat for cooking.

When cooking at the hearth, it is possible to employ all of the cooking methods you use with a modern stove. If you acquire the knowledge that allows you to select the correct pot or utensil, to control the intensity of your fire and to judge how close to the fire to place the pot, you will be ready to cook many delicious meals.

To Fire the Oven

In many early American homes, the oven was constructed as part of the fireplace having an opening about waist high. The fire is laid on the floor of the oven. Crumple newspaper or arrange wood shavings on the oven floor. Set small pieces of kindling over or near the paper. Light the newspaper, adding more kindling as necessary. When the kindling is burning, begin to add larger pieces of wood, moving them to the back of the oven and adding more until the floor is covered with burning wood. After about two hours, test to determine if the oven is hot enough for baking. The testing is done by throwing a small amount of flour in the oven. If it browns without burning in half a minute, it is ready. Use a special coal rake to gather the coals to the front of the oven where they can then be shoveled onto the hearth for use in cooking. If the coals are not needed at the time, they can be raked through a hole in the floor of the oven

4

and will fall into the ash pit below.

If bread is to be baked on the bare floor, the oven must be scrubbed with a long-handled mop. Food which requires high heat such as pie, bread, and biscuits is baked right away. In about 30 minutes the heat will have fallen enough for cakes. When the oven cools to low, puddings and custards are baked.

An outside bake oven is heated just as the kitchen one is and the coals are raked into the ash pit.

The museum where I work and teach does not have a bake oven. The baking methods which are employed are: the **Dutch Oven**, the **Tin Biscuit Oven**, and the **Hanging Griddle**.

The **Dutch Oven** is the most versatile of all hearth cooking equipment. If it were the only pot one owned, wonderful meals could still be prepared. This iron kettle with three short legs also can be used to stew or fry meat or vegetables. The kettle is fitted with a lid with a recessed top to hold coals. If using the Dutch oven for all of your baking, it is convenient to have several sizes, but if you are limited to only one, choose a medium size.

To use your **Dutch Oven** for **baking**, select a spot on or near your hearth which will not be in your main path as you move around preparing your meal. In order to conserve coals, preheat your oven near the fire with the lid propped against it. Put three good-sized shovelfuls of coals on the spot which has been selected for baking. Be sure that the coals are clear orangy-red. If they are smoking, wait a few minutes until they reach the proper heat to put them in place for the baking. Move the oven to the pile of coals. Place the food to be baked in the oven, setting it on a trivet or several small rocks. This will allow the hot air to surround the food. Cover the oven and put three shovelfuls of properly heated coals on the recessed lid. The coals beneath the oven and on top of the lid should be insulated with a light layer of ashes. If the food to be baked requires a high temperature, change the coals after about 15 minutes. If the food needs a longer baking period at a low temperature, you can wait about 45 minutes before changing the coals.

A **Biscuit Oven**, being made of tin, **bakes** with the heat from the fire and the reflection of the fire off the tin. This oven (see illustration page 12) can be used to bake not only biscuits but also cookies and small pies. The food to be baked is placed on the oven shelf and the oven is then set with the open side toward the fire. The food is allowed to bake until done and browned.

Biscuits, scones, crumpets, and English muffins are among the breads which can be **baked** on a **griddle**. The griddle is hung from the crane and the height from the fire is adjusted according to the bread which is being prepared. Denser or heavier bread requires more heat to bake.

Roasting is cooking with dry heat. The most common method for roasting at the hearth is to skewer the meat on a spit which is rested on andirons equipped with holders for the spit. A drip pan, usually made of tin, is placed beneath the meat to catch the drippings which are then used for basting the roasting meat or for gravy. (sketch page 11).

For **roasting** small game, fowl, or small cuts of meat, a **Reflector Oven**, or **Tin Kitchen**, is a useful item. The heat reflected by the tin, in addition to the direct heat from the fire, cuts down on the amount of time required for roasting. The roasting oven (see illustration page 11) is set with the open side facing the fire. The curved bottom of the oven catches and holds the drippings which can be poured off by means of a spout on the side. The oven is equipped with a small door on the closed side which can be utilized for checking and basting the meat without moving it away from the fire.

Two distinctive types of roasters used on the hearth are the **Bird Roaster**, (see illustration page 13) which was used for **roasting** bobwhites (quail) and the **Apple Roaster** (see illustration page 14). I have reproductions in my collection and use them quite frequently with good results.

If possible, the fireplace should be equipped with a swinging iron crane. Food to be **stewed**, **boiled**, or **steamed** is hung in iron pots from the crane by hooks, trammels, or ratchets. This crane is much safer and more convenient than the lug pole, a green stake which was placed in the fireplace to hold pots above the fire for cooking in early cabins.

When **boiling**, **simmering**, or **steaming** food, the speed and energy with which the food cooks is determined by the position of the pot on the crane with relation to the fire, and by the intensity of the fire.

For **boiling** food or liquid rapidly, arrange the iron pot directly above the fire, hanging it low or near the fire. The pot should be checked frequently to determine the amount of the liquid contents as food boils dry quite rapidly over an open fire.

In **simmering**, the pot should be moved to the end of the crane, away from the center of the fire. The pot should be hung high. If necessary, rearrange the coals in order to lower the heat beneath the pot.

Steaming is accomplished by setting a tightly closed pudding mold on a rack in a large pot. Boiling water is added to come half way up the side of the mold. Cover the pot and hang it on the end of the crane away from the center of the fire. The water should be kept steaming but not allowed to boil.

Frying is done by hanging a large pot of fat from the crane. The pot is hung over direct heat and the temperature of the fat must be kept very high to fry effectively. Be extremely careful when handling pots containing hot fat, which is highly combustible.

A **Spider** is a heavy iron, long-handled pan which is equipped with three legs to stand over coals piled on the hearth. It is used for **frying** and **sauteing** food. A **frying pan**, or **skillet**, preferably long handled, is placed on a trivet over the pile of coals for frying or sauteing.

A **Gridiron** is used for **broiling**. It is made of heavy iron and could be ordered from the blacksmith. The gridiron is placed over a small bed of hot coals. When the gridiron is heated, the meat to be cooked is placed on it and allowed to cook until it reaches the preferred state of doneness.

Some foods can be cooked directly on the hearth or in the hot ashes. Corn pones can be placed on the warm, cleanly swept hearth, covered by warm ashes and baked until done. The pones are then removed and the ashes brushed off. If necessary, the ashes can be wiped off with a damp cloth. Sometimes the pones are baked, carefully wrapped in a cabbage leaf. Sweet or Irish potatoes can be washed and dried and then buried in warm ashes to bake until soft. These methods for baking were used long before the first pot was formed.

Hearth cooking requires some essential tools, among which are tongs and a shovel. Long-handled spoons and forks are needed; skimmers and turners are handy to have. There are many types of pots, utensils, tools, and equipment that are useful and fun to collect.

Old pots and pans suitable for cooking at the hearth can sometimes be found in antique or junk shops. It is important that such equipment be cleaned in very hot water with soap. After rinsing and drying carefully, if there are any rust spots, you can remove them by lightly rubbing the equipment with fine steel wool.

New or newly cleaned ironware must be "seasoned." This is accomplished by applying, inside and outside, a thin coat of shortening. The pot is then placed in a warm oven and left until the oven is completely cold. If working at a hearth where there is no oven, the greased pan can be hung over a very low fire until thoroughly heated and then allowed to cool. If properly seasoned, after use the pot need only be well-rinsed and thoroughly dried. The best way to be sure that the clean pot is completely dry is to set it beside the dying fire for a while. Never leave food or liquid in an iron pot.

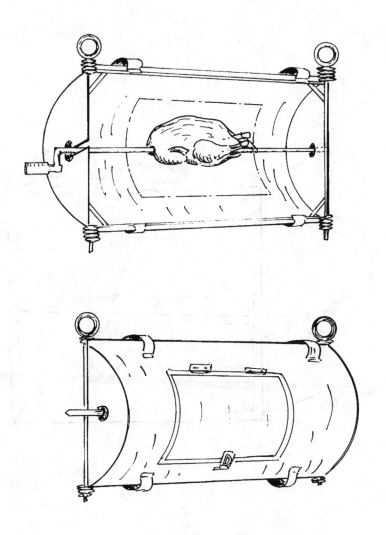

Reflector Oven, sometimes called Tin Kitchen

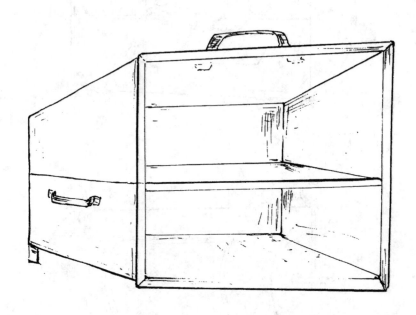

Tin Biscuit Oven

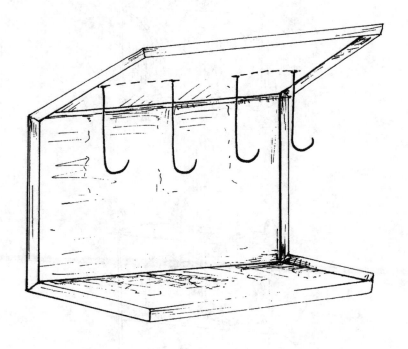

Tin Bird Roaster

13

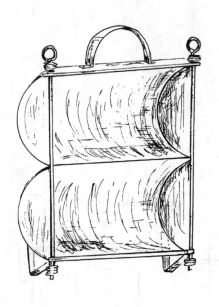

Apple Roaster

Part One: Soups and Chowders

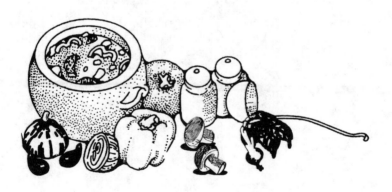

BEAN WITH HAM HOCKS SOUP

Beans which had been carefully dried during the hot summer months were often served as a pot of wonderful winter soup, simmered to perfection over the same fire which provided warmth to the colonist's cabin.

1 pound dried beans
2 ham hocks or leftover ham bone with some meat
1 pod dried red pepper
2 tablespoons butter
1 large onion, diced
several sprigs of savory
salt and freshly ground pepper

Soak beans overnight in cool water. Drain, then rinse several times to whiten. Place beans, ham hocks, and pepper pod in large pot. Add 3 quarts of water.

HEARTH METHOD: Hang pot on crane over brisk fire. When the pot begins to boil, move it to the end of the crane and let simmer until the beans are done, about one hour.

Melt the butter in a spider or frying pan placed over coals on the hearth. Add onions and cook until transparent. Add cooked onions, savory, and salt and pepper to beans and allow to cook for about 15 minutes to wed the flavors.

Remove meat from ham hocks, dice, and return to pot.

MODERN METHOD: Follow the hearth directions, simmering the soup over low heat. Saute the onions in skillet over moderate heat.

Serve in large soup plates with a wedge of cornbread for a delicious meal.

SPICED CARROT SOUP

The carrot was a popular vegetable in early America because it could be stored in the root cellar or buried in the ground below the freeze line for use during the long winter months.

2 tablespoons butter
2 cups milk
1 large onion, finely chopped
several sprigs of thyme or 1/2 teaspoon dried thyme
4 medium sized potatoes, diced
1/2 teaspoon pepper sauce (see recipe on page 154)
12 carrots, finely diced
6 cups homemade chicken broth
2 bay leaves
1/2 teaspoon sugar
1 cup light cream
1/2 teaspoon salt
freshly ground pepper

HEARTH METHOD: Melt the butter in large pot hung from crane. Saute onion in butter and then add the diced potatoes, carrots, chicken broth, and bay leaves. Cook until the vegetables are tender. Add cream, milk, thyme, pepper sauce, sugar, salt, and pepper and heat to boiling point. Remove the bay leaves.

MODERN METHOD: Saute onions, then cook vegetables over moderate heat, following hearth method. If desired, vegetables can be pureed in blender when done. Be sure to remove bay leaves before blending.

Serve soup garnished with fresh thyme.

CORN CHOWDER 78896

Soon after the colonists were introduced to maize by the Indians, they started combining it with pork to make a delicious and satisfying chowder.

1/2 pound salt pork, diced
1 onion, sliced
1 quart water
3 potatoes, sliced
2 cups green corn, freshly cut from cob
6 common crackers, soaked in water
1 cup hot milk
2 tablespoons butter
1/2 teaspoon salt, if necessary
1/4 teaspoon pepper, freshly ground
    thyme, several sprigs fresh
    or 1/2 teaspoon dried

HEARTH METHOD: Brown diced pork in large pot hung from crane. Add sliced onions and when they are translucent, add the quart of water. Add the potatoes and corn and cook for about 30 minutes. Add crackers, milk, butter, salt, pepper, and thyme. Cook for an additional 15 minutes.

MODERN METHOD: Prepare as in hearth method, cooking over low heat.

SUMMERTIME CRAB SOUP

Crab soup was a summertime favorite among settlers along the shore. In those early times before refrigeration, people did not understand that it was the heat associated with a thunderstorm that would spoil soup. Consequently, it was the custom to throw the soup away if thunder was heard.

1 pound beef, cubed
1/4 pound salt pork, diced
2 quarts of water
vegetables as available, including onions,
     potatoes, beans, okra, carrots, cabbages, peas, celery,
     tomatoes
6 small crabs, cleaned and quartered
herbs including thyme, parsley, marjoram
salt and freshly ground pepper

HEARTH METHOD: Brown the beef and pork in a large soup pot hung from crane. Add water and thoroughly cook meat. Add the prepared vegetables and simmer all until done. Add crabs, herbs and seasonings and cook for 15 additional minutes.

MODERN METHOD: Prepare as in hearth method, cooking over moderate heat.

BLACK IRON POT FISH CHOWDER

This chowder can be made with almost any kind of fish—salt or fresh water—and although it seems to taste better made in an old black pot, it can be prepared in a modern one.

8 slices of salt pork
4 pounds of firm fish, cut in slices
3 medium onions, thinly sliced
3 medium potatoes, sliced
8 seafood crackers
1/2 teaspoon salt, if necessary
1/4 teaspoon pepper, freshly ground
    thyme, several sprigs fresh or 1/2 teaspoon dried
1 lemon, thinly sliced
water, level with contents of pot

HEARTH METHOD: Brown pork in soup pot hung from crane. Take pot off crane and remove browned pork. In pot, layer fish, pork, onions, potatoes, and crackers, sprinkling each layer with salt, pepper, and thyme and adding the lemon slices. Add water to a level even with the contents of the pot. Replace pot on crane and cover closely. Do not remove the lid until the chowder is nearly done, after about one hour. Test for taste and doneness.

MODERN METHOD: Follow directions in hearth method, cooking the chowder over low heat.

CREAMY CRAB SOUP

This elegant and very rich soup should be served in small portions. Stick with these few ingredients and do not add too much flour; you want the soup to be creamy and thick but not pasty.

2 tablespoons butter
1 1/2 tablespoons flour
3 cups milk
salt and freshly ground pepper
cayenne pepper
1 pound fresh crab meat
1 cup heavy cream
1 hard boiled egg, finely chopped
sherry, if desired

HEARTH METHOD: Place soup pot on trivet over pile of coals on hearth. Melt butter in pot and stir in flour. Stir until well-mixed being careful not to burn. Add milk, then the seasonings. When mixture begins to thicken and is heated, add the fresh crab meat and the heavy cream. At this point, the finely chopped egg can be mixed in the soup or the soup can be served with the egg sprinkled on top. Stir in sherry, if desired, or serve sherry on the side.

MODERN METHOD: Prepare soup as in hearth method, cooking over low heat.

For color, sprinkle soup with small amount of cayenne pepper before serving.

OYSTER BISQUE

With an abundance of available oysters and after dairy herds were established, the colonists were able to enjoy this tasty dish made rich with butter, cream, and milk.

1 quart milk
1 quart oysters, minced
6 tablespoons butter

5 tablespoons flour
salt and freshly ground pepper
2 cups heavy cream

HEARTH METHOD: Heat milk in pot hung from crane. Scald oysters in their own liquor in a spider or skillet; set over a pile of coals on hearth. Add liquor to the heated milk. Place clean spider on coals and melt butter. Blend in the flour and add to hot milk mixture. Add the seasonings, stir in the oysters and cream, heating thoroughly. Do not boil.

MODERN METHOD: Follow directions in hearth method, cooking over low heat.

PEA SOUP WITH HAM

1 pound dried peas, soaked overnight
1 slice ham or ham bone with some meat
3 quarts water
1 large onion diced
2 stalks celery, diced
salt and freshly ground pepper

HEARTH METHOD: Put all ingredients in pot and hang from crane. Cook slowly, over low flame, for about two hours or until the peas are done and the soup is thick. Mashing the vegetables slightly with a potato masher will thicken soup.

MODERN METHOD: Follow the hearth method for preparation of the soup and cook on medium heat.

HERB GARDEN SORREL SOUP

French sorrel (Rumex scutatus) is a hardy perennial which is a nice addition to the herb garden. It has a pleasant, though slightly sour taste which is delicious when used in soup or sauce.

2 tablespoons butter
4 cups sorrel leaves, shredded
3 medium potatoes, diced in small pieces
6 cups homemade chicken broth
whipped, unsweetened cream
chopped chives

HEARTH METHOD: Wash the sorrel thoroughly. Melt butter in pot hung from crane over low flame. Add the shredded sorrel leaves and diced potatoes. Cook until the sorrel leaves are wilted, about 6 minutes. Add the chicken broth and simmer for 25 minutes.

MODERN METHOD: Follow the hearth method, cooking over moderate heat.

Serve garnished with the unsweetened whipped cream sprinkled with chopped chives.

TOMATO BISQUE

The tomato originated in Central and South America and was taken back to Europe by explorers. Tomatoes were grown by Jefferson as early as 1781, and at the beginning of the 19th century, the general populace had decided that tomatoes were not poisonous and consumed them in goodly quantities.

1 quart tomatoes
1 large onion, finely diced
2 stalks celery, finely diced
parsley, several sprigs
2 cups homemade beef stock
5 whole cloves
1/4 teaspoon salt
1/4 teaspoon pepper,
    freshly ground
1 teaspoon sugar
1 tablespoon butter
1 tablespoon flour
2 cups light cream

HEARTH METHOD: In pot over medium flame, gently cook tomatoes, onions, celery, parsley and stock for one hour. If desired, soup can be put through a strainer. Add cloves, salt, pepper, and sugar. Thicken by adding butter which has been rolled in flour. Add the cream and heat to just under the boiling point.

MODERN METHOD: Follow hearth method, cook over moderate heat. Be careful not to boil.

To garnish, sprinkle with minced parsley.

Part Two:
Savory Creations

BEEFSTEAK PUDDING

Fruit, meat, vegetables, whatever was available was made into pudding in early American homes. Because older cows were usually the ones butchered, beef at that time was very tough. This recipe is a good way to use tough beef.

2 medium onions, sliced
3 tablespoons butter
2 pounds round steak,
   cut in slices
2 cups homemade beef broth

1/2 teaspoon salt
1/4 teaspoon pepper, freshly
   ground
2 tablespoons butter
2 tablespoons flour

HEARTH METHOD: In spider placed over coals on hearth, cook onions in butter. Add meat and brown well. Pour in the broth and then add the seasonings. Cover the spider and simmer until the meat is tender.

Roll butter in flour and stir into spider contents to thicken. Set spider aside.

MODERN METHOD: Following hearth method, prepare beefsteak mixture in skillet over medium heat.

PUDDING BATTER

2 cups flour
1 teaspoon salt
4 eggs

2 cups milk
2 tablespoons butter

In a bowl mix flour and salt. Beat eggs slightly and add to milk. Make well in flour mixture and pour in the milk and egg mixture. Beat until smooth.

HEARTH METHOD: Place pudding pan in heated Dutch oven and set over bed of coals. Add butter to pudding pan and when it has melted, pour in half the pudding mixture. Cover the oven

—Beefsteak Pudding Batter continued

and bake the mixture for about 15 minutes at which time the batter should be nicely puffed. Spread the hot beefsteak mixture over the pudding mixture and then cover with the remaining batter mixture. Cover the oven and place coals on top. Continue to bake for an additional 15 minutes or until the pudding is brown and done.

MODERN METHOD: Melt the butter in ovenproof dish in oven which has been preheated to 400 degrees. Follow the hearth method for baking the pudding.

Pudding should be served immediately.

POT ROAST WITH HERBS AND VEGETABLES

The flavor of a pot roast with vegetables is much improved by adding a variety of herbs selected from the herb garden. If fresh herbs are not available, dried ones can be used.

2 tablespoons butter
2 medium onions, diced
1/2 teaspoon salt
1/4 teaspoon pepper, freshly ground
pot roast, about 5 pounds
3 cups homemade beef broth
1 bay leaf
8 pearl onions
5 carrots cut in large pieces
2 stalks celery cut in large pieces
4 small new potatoes
herbs: marjoram, rosemary, savory, thyme, parsley. Use any
    one or a combination of several.

HEARTH METHOD: Hang large pot over medium fire. Melt butter and cook the diced onions until transparent. Rub salt and pepper into meat and then brown with cooked onions. Add half the broth and the bay leaf, and cook for about two hours.

Add the vegetables and the remainder of the broth and cook until almost done. At this point, add the herbs and continue to cook for about 15 minutes or until the vegetables are done. If necessary, the gravy can be thickened by rubbing 1 tablespoon of butter in 1 tablespoon of flour and adding to liquid in pot.

MODERN METHOD: Follow hearth method, placing large pot over medium heat.

TIN KITCHEN ROAST BEEF
WITH POTATOES UNDER

The tin kitchen, which was in use in America as early as the end of the 1700s, is a wonderful way to roast meat. The meat is roasted by the combination of the heat from the fire and the reflection from the tin. Potatoes can be roasted underneath, gaining flavor from the meat drippings which collect.

6 to 8-pound roast
salt and freshly ground pepper
flour
herb of choice: sage, thyme, marjoram or rosemary
red wine
potatoes - 1 for each person, all same size

HEARTH METHOD: Rub meat with salt, pepper, flour, and the herb. Skewer the roast to spit securing with butcher's twine if necessary. Place spit in oven and position the oven near the fire. Baste frequently with drippings and red wine. Roast for about 15 minutes per pound.

Peel potatoes, leaving whole, or if desired, leave unpeeled. Place in pot and cover with water. Hang the pot over fire and cook until potatoes are half done. Remove potatoes from pot, drain, and place under roast. Turn and baste with the drippings until potatoes are brown and done.

MODERN METHOD: Follow hearth method, roasting the meat in a preheated 350° oven.

Place the half-cooked potatoes around roast and continue to roast until the potatoes are done.

Serve the roast on a large platter surrounded by the potatoes. Drippings from roast can be ladled over the meat and potatoes. Garnish with sprigs of the herb with which roast was cooked.

TASTY ROASTED BIRDS

Small tin bird roasters (see illustration page 13) were commonly seen in early kitchens to roast bobwhites (quail) or other birds. The roaster has a flat, upright face with narrow side projections and a base with turned-up edges where bread was placed to catch the drippings. Wire hooks were attached on the inside and from the back, a handle projected on which the roaster sat or stood in front of the fire. These roasters are rare today but are a delight to use and a lovely addition to hearth cooking equipment collections.

bobwhite (quail) 1 per person, at least
salt and pepper, freshly ground
flour and butter

HEARTH METHOD: After cleaning the birds, rub well with salt and pepper. Hang birds by breast bone on hooks. Set roaster in front of fire, basting birds frequently with water and salt mixture. When the birds are almost done, begin to baste with butter and flour which have been rubbed together.

Serve on toast, with gravy made from drippings, poured over the bird.

If you do not have a bird roaster, place the seasoned birds in a dish in a preheated Dutch oven. Place oven on coals and put coals on top of lid. Allow to cook for about 25 minutes, basting with butter and flour as necessary.

A third method for cooking is to attach the birds to the spit of the reflector oven in the usual manner and roast, turning and basting, for about 15-20 minutes until done.

MODERN METHOD: Roast seasoned birds in 350°F oven until browned and done. Birds should be basted frequently. Serve as above.

RABBIT FRICASSEE WITH RICE

Rabbit was frequently served in early American homes because it was plentiful and easily obtained. The gravy, or sauce, is delicious served over rice.

1 rabbit cut in serving pieces
1/2 teaspoon salt
1/4 teaspoon pepper, freshly ground
2 tablespoons butter
2 cups homemade chicken broth
1 tablespoon butter
2 tablespoons flour
1/2 cup light cream
1/2 teaspoon savory
1/4 teaspoon nutmeg, freshly ground
1/4 teaspoon mace

HEARTH METHOD: Rub meat with salt and pepper. Melt butter in spider placed over coals on hearth and brown meat well. Remove the browned meat from the pan and pour off the drippings. Return meat to pan. Add the chicken broth, cover and return to the coals. Simmer, turning occasionally until tender, about 30-40 minutes.

Rub butter into flour and stir into mixture. Stir in cream, add savory, nutmeg, and mace and cook uncovered for about 5 minutes or until flavors have mingled.

MODERN METHOD: Follow the hearth method, browning the meat in a skillet over high heat. Cook over medium heat until tender.

To serve, put mound of rice (recipe page 86) on plate with a piece of the cooked rabbit along side. Spoon on gravy.

FRONTIER FRIED SQUIRREL AND GRAVY

Squirrels provided a tasty addition to the diet of the pioneers on the frontier. Squirrel could be served at any meal and often an early-rising sharpshooter would secure enough squirrels for a delicious breakfast.

2 squirrels cut in serving pieces
salt and freshly ground pepper
flour
3 tablespoons lard
2 cups water

HEARTH METHOD: The squirrels should be parboiled before frying. Place squirrels in pan, add cold water to barely cover. Set pan on trivet over coals, or hang the pot from crane. Allow to boil gently for about 10 minutes or until the meat is barely tender. Remove meat from water and dry.

Rub the meat with seasonings and flour. Heat lard in spider over coals piled on hearth. Fry the squirrel in the melted lard until golden brown. Remove meat and pour off all except 2 tablespoons of the drippings. Add the water and bring to a boil. Return the squirrel to the spider, cover, and cook over low coal heat for about one hour, turning the meat occasionally.

MODERN METHOD: Prepare as in hearth cooking method, cooking the squirrel over low heat for about one hour.

Serve the squirrel and gravy over hot buttermilk biscuits.

HERB-BRAISED LEG OF
LAMB WITH VEGETABLES

This lamb is truly delicious when cooked in an iron pot over a wood fire. The flavor is enhanced by the fresh herbs.

3 tablespoons butter
leg of lamb
6 carrots
3 onions, medium, quartered
3 cloves garlic
2 cups meat stock, homemade
1/2 cup Madeira
fresh herbs: rosemary, marjoram, thyme
1/2 teaspoon salt
1/4 teaspoon pepper, freshly ground
1 tablespoon flour
1/4 cup water

HEARTH METHOD: Melt the butter in large pot hung over a brisk fire; add lamb. Brown the lamb, turning frequently. When sufficiently browned, remove from pot. Brown the vegetables and garlic in the same butter. Replace lamb on top of vegetables and add the stock and wine. Cover the pot closely and move it from center of fire to end of crane. Baste frequently with broth in pot. When the meat is tender, season with the herbs, salt and pepper. Allow to cook for a few more minutes and then remove the meat and vegetables from the pan. Strain juices, skimming off excess fat. Combine the flour with the water and stir into gravy to thicken.

MODERN METHOD: Follow hearth method, cooking meat over moderate heat.

Serve the lamb on platter surrounded by the vegetables. Garnish with more fresh herbs.

ROAST SPRING LEG OF LAMB WITH ROSEMARY

Lamb seems to have an affinity for rosemary and both the taste and aroma of the lamb are improved by this addition. Be sure to have a hardy rosemary plant growing in your garden or a tender variety in a sunny window to provide this versatile herb when needed.

leg of lamb
several sprigs of rosemary
salt and freshly ground pepper

HEARTH METHOD: With a very sharp knife make deep gashes over the surface of the lamb. Push sprigs of rosemary into these openings. Rub the lamb with the seasonings. Run the spit through the center of the meat against the bone and place skewers to secure in place. Put spit in reflector oven and set it near the fire. Roast for about 25 minutes per pound, basting frequently with the drippings.

MODERN METHOD: Follow hearth method, roasting the meat in a preheated 325°F oven for about 25 minutes per pound.

Serve the leg of lamb on a platter garnished with fresh sprigs of rosemary with a boat of gravy alongside.

BACKBONE WITH DUMPLINGS

Pork backbone, either fresh or "salted down," provided the basis for a good, nourishing meal whether cooked with greens or dumplings. Try this dish on a cold wintry day!

mess* fresh or salted backbone, about 2 pounds
salt (if needed) and freshly ground pepper
pod red pepper
1 gallon of water
1/2 teaspoon sage, fresh or dried

HEARTH METHOD: If using salted meat, wash several times in cold water. Put the backbones, salt, peppers, and about one gallon of water in large pot. Hang pot from crane.

Cook until meat is done and falling from bones and water is reduced to about half. Add the sage and cook for a few minutes to mingle flavors.

Drop dumpling mixture in pieces about the size of a walnut into the boiling backbone pot. Cover pot. Let boil rapidly for about 10 minutes without uncovering the pot.

MODERN METHOD: Follow the directions for hearth cooking simmering the meat over low heat. Cook dumplings over high heat.

Serve with plenty of hot cornbread.

DUMPLINGS

2 cups flour
4 teaspoons baking powder
1 teaspoon salt
1 cup milk

Combine the dry ingredients and mix into a dough by stirring the milk into the mixture. With a fork and spoon drop the dumplings into the backbone pot.

NOTE: *Mess is an old-fashioned designation for a quantity of food sufficient for a dish or a single occasion.

FRESH BOILED HAM

With a prepared ham on hand, you are ready to serve many different and delicious meals. Sliced as part of a meal, in made dishes or served in sandwiches, ham is the pride of the cook.

medium-sized fresh ham
2 tablespoons mustard
2 tablespoons brown sugar

HEARTH METHOD: Put washed and cleaned ham in large pot and cover with cold water. Hang pot away from the middle of the fire. Bring pot slowly to boil and let simmer until done, allowing about 20 minutes per pound. (Ham is done when small bone can be easily removed.) Remove from fire and let ham cool completely in the liquid. Remove and drain. The ham is now ready for sandwiches or to be sliced as an ingredient for a made dish.

If to be presented whole, the ham should be browned. Skin and score the ham. Rub with a mixture of prepared mustard and brown sugar. Put ham on spit, skewer, put spit in reflector oven and place near fire. Baste ham with drippings, turning frequently until is it nicely browned.

MODERN METHOD: Prepare ham as in hearth method, simmering ham on low heat.

To brown the ham for serving whole, prepare as for hearth method. Place ham in preheated 350°F oven and bake until nicely browned, basting frequently.

COUNTRY HAM WITH REDEYE GRAVY

Country hams from specially fed hogs, cured and smoked, and served with redeye gravy poured over hot grits and buttermilk biscuits—what breakfast memories come forth to cheer us with thoughts of home.

country ham, sliced 1/2 inch thick
1/2 cup cold water
2 tablespoons strong coffee

HEARTH METHOD: Fry the ham in spider placed over coals on hearth. Turn to brown on both sides. Remove the browned ham to warmed platter. Pour off drippings except for about 2 tablespoons. Pour in the water and coffee and bring to boil. Remove from fire.

MODERN METHOD: Prepare the ham and gravy as in hearth method, cooking over medium heat.

Serve the ham with the gravy poured over or served alongside in a boat.

LOIN ROAST OF PORK WITH THYME

Thyme, used in this recipe, is a hardy little perennial, a lovely addition to the herb garden, providing flavor to food and substance for the bees hovering around the plants. Other herbs which are good with pork include sage and rosemary.

pork loin roast, 4-5 pounds
salt and freshly ground pepper
2 tablespoons flour
thyme, several sprigs fresh or 1/2 teaspoon dried

HEARTH METHOD: Rub meat with mixture of salt, pepper, flour and thyme. Put roast on spit and place in reflector oven, set in front of a brisk fire. Turn and baste often with the drippings. Roast for about two hours or until the juices run clear.

MODERN METHOD: Follow hearth method for preparing roast. Place in roasting pan with fat side up. Put pan in preheated 400°F oven and bake until done, about two hours or until the juices run clear.

Serve the roast on a large platter garnished with fresh sprigs of thyme.

FRIED SALT PORK WITH MILK GRAVY

Salt pork was probably the most important food used in early kitchens. It was not only used to season but was sometimes the only meat that pioneers would have all winter. It is very tasty and will add flavor to everything from chowder to fried apples.

salt pork, thickly sliced, about 3 slices per person
corn meal
pepper, freshly ground
2 tablespoons lard
2 tablespoons flour
2 cups milk

HEARTH METHOD: Place spider over heap of coals on hearth. Put pork in spider and add water to cover. Bring to boil and continue cooking for 2 minutes to remove salt. Remove meat and discard water. Dip the slices in cornmeal; dust with pepper. Melt lard in spider, add pork and fry until golden brown, turning once.

To make gravy, pour off drippings leaving about 2 tablespoons in spider. Add 2 tablespoons flour to drippings and brown, stirring to prevent burning. Add two cups of milk. Stir and cook until smooth and sufficiently thick. Add freshly ground pepper to taste.

MODERN METHOD: Follow hearth method, cooking meat in skillet over medium high heat. Cook the gravy over medium heat.

Serve the meat and gravy with rice, mashed potatoes, hot cornbread or biscuits.

SAUSAGE PATTIES WITH APPLES

1 pound sausage meat formed into patties
cooking apples cored and quartered, but not peeled
brown sugar, about 1 tablespoon
cinnamon (if desired)

HEARTH METHOD: Put the patties in cold spider which is then placed on small heap of coals on hearth. Cook slowly until the patties are browned and the center is done. Pour off most of the drippings. Add the prepared apples and cover the pan. Sprinkle the apples with brown sugar and continue to cook covered until the apples are tender and almost done. Remove the cover and continue to cook in order to glaze the apples. Apples can be sprinkled with cinnamon if desired.

MODERN METHOD: Follow hearth method, cooking sausage patties over low heat until browned and well done. Add the prepared apples and continue to cook over low heat until done and glazed.

If you are using bought sausage meat rather than homemade, it can be spiced up by the addition of red pepper flakes and dried rubbed sage.

CHICKEN WITH DUMPLINGS

It was customary to serve rolled dumplings with chicken in my family and Auntie's were the best! It is important that the pot not be uncovered while the dumplings are cooking, ensuring that they will be light and delicious.

4-5 pounds stewing chicken
several sprigs parsley
2 stalks celery
1 onion
salt and freshly ground pepper
cold water to cover

HEARTH METHOD: Put chicken in pot, add remaining ingredients, cover with cold water. Cover pot and hang over medium fire. Simmer for about one hour (or longer if necessary, depending on the age of the chicken) or until chicken is tender. Remove chicken and vegetables from broth. Discard vegetables. Bone chicken, if desired, and return to pot.

Set pot back over the fire and return to boiling point. Drop the dumplings in the boiling liquid, cover, and cook for 10 minutes. Do not peek!

MODERN METHOD: Follow hearth method, cooking chicken over medium heat. Raise heat to cook the dumplings.

ROLLED DUMPLINGS

2 cups flour   1/3 cup lard
2 teaspoons baking powder   1/2 cup milk
1 teaspoon salt

Combine flour, baking powder, and salt. Cut in the lard. Add milk to make a stiff dough. Roll out on a floured board to 1/8 inch thickness and cut in strips or squares.

COUNTRY CAPTAIN

The creation of this dish may have happened on a merchant ship returning from the East Indies carrying a load of spices plus live chickens to be cooked as food for the crew. The captain added some of his exotic cargo to the chicken meat, thereby creating Country Captain.

1 teaspoon salt
1/2 teaspoon pepper, freshly ground
1 1/2 teaspoons curry powder
1/2 cup flour
1/2 cup butter
2-3 pound chickens, cut in serving pieces
1 medium onion, chopped
1 green pepper, chopped
thyme, several sprigs fresh or 1/2 teaspoon dried
3 fresh garden tomatoes, quartered
1/2 cup golden raisins
1/2 cup almonds, sliced

HEARTH METHOD: Add the salt, pepper and curry powder to the flour and mix well. Roll the chicken pieces in the flour until well coated.

Heat the butter in a spider placed over heap of coals on hearth. Add the chicken and brown until golden, turn, brown other side, and remove from pan.

Put the onion, green pepper, thyme, and tomatoes into the spider and slowly cook for 5 minutes, stirring.

Put the chicken back in the pan, cover and cook over slow coals for 45 minutes. Put the chicken on warm platter and set in warm place.

Stir the golden raisins and sliced almonds into the vegetables in the spider, allowing to simmer, uncovered, for five minutes. Pour over the chicken and serve accompanied by rice. (page 86).

MODERN METHOD: Follow hearth method, browning chicken in skillet placed over high heat. Lower heat and cook onions, green pepper, thyme, and tomatoes. Continue to cook the chicken over medium heat.

A good dish to serve to a large crowd.

REAL CHICKEN PIE

This was the pie which was prepared for "dinner on the ground," that marvelous spread which usually followed a "graveyard working" or which provided a noontime repast at an "all day's singing." The pie is made by filling a pastry-lined baking dish with layers of cooked chicken, sliced boiled eggs, strips of pastry, and a rich sauce and covering with a pastry strip top. Do not add vegetables to this pie.

1 chicken
water to cover
1/2 teaspoon salt
1/4 teaspoon pepper, freshly ground

HEARTH METHOD: Place the chicken in pot and barely cover with water. Add salt and pepper. Hang covered pot on crane over low fire and simmer until tender, about 1 hour. When done, remove pot from heat and let chicken cool in broth. Remove chicken from bones and set aside.

MODERN METHOD: Follow hearth method, simmering chicken over low fire until tender.

BOILED EGGS

2 eggs
water to cover

HEARTH METHOD: Place eggs in small pot and cover with cold water. Hang pot on spit over moderate fire. Let eggs boil for about 10 minutes. Remove from pot and place in pan of cold water to cool. When cool, peel, and slice.

MODERN METHOD: Follow hearth directions, cooking over low heat.

PASTRY

(This recipe makes enough pastry for two ordinary pies, but this chicken pie will require the entire amount).

1/2 teaspoon salt
2 1/2 cups flour
8 tablespoons lard
3 tablespoons cold water

HEARTH AND MODERN METHOD: Prepare pastry by mixing salt with flour. Cut in half (4 tablespoons) of the lard until mixture resembles meal. Add water, a tablespoon at a time, lightly mixing with a fork. Divide the pastry into two parts. Roll out one piece quite thin. Line sides and bottom of pudding dish. Cut the remainder of the lard into the remaining portion of pastry. Roll out pastry and cut into strips.

SAUCE

Stock from chicken
2 tablespoons flour
1 cup cream

HEARTH METHOD: Mix a small portion of the cooled stock with the flour. Put this mixture in a spider over coals and add enough additional stock for about 2 cups. Test to see if salt and pepper are needed. Cook and stir the sauce until smooth and thickened. Add cream and mix well.

MODERN METHOD: Follow hearth method, cooking sauce over low heat.

TO ASSEMBLE PIE

Set out:
    lined pudding dish
    chicken, cooked, removed from bones but left in large pieces
    eggs, boiled, sliced
    1/4 pound butter
    pastry strips
    prepared sauce

Into the lined pudding dish, put a layer of chicken, sliced eggs, dot with butter. Cover the chicken with strips of pastry. Repeat layers until all ingredients are used, saving enough strips of pastry for top of pie. Pour in the amount of sauce needed to fill the dish. Top with remaining pastry strips.

HEARTH METHOD: Set the pudding dish in a preheated Dutch oven and bake for about 45 minutes, adding coals as necessary, until center of pie is done and the top is browned.

MODERN METHOD: Place prepared pie in preheated 450° oven and bake for 15 minutes. Reduce temperature to 350° and bake for an additional 30 minutes until center is done and the top is brown.

NOTE: "Dinner on the ground" is a picnic-type meal served on tablecloths or quilts spread on the church grounds. Sometimes the church pews were carried outdoors and used as tables. Some churches had tables made by placing boards between trees, held in place by wooden cleats nailed on the trees. Even when pews or board tables were used, it was still called "dinner on the ground." These dinners were usually held in the country where the church was built among magnificent trees.

In the days when perpetual care was not provided and

cemeteries were located beside the church, each family tended its own plot. A day (usually Decoration Day), would be designated for all the families to come and clean the graves. If there were plots owned by families who had moved away or all members of the family had "died off," when the participants had finished their own plots, together, they cleaned all the remaining ones. There was a break at noon to enjoy together the dinner which they had brought. These "graveyard workings" provided a time for catching up on news and gossip, seeing members of extended families, and fellowship and togetherness.

"All day singings" were a time for entertainment and fun. A special day, usually Sunday, was decided upon and the word was spread. Groups of gospel singers, including duets, trios, quartets, and choruses, with their accompanists, would meet at the church early in the morning.

All day the groups would take turns entertaining the crowd with gospel music or old hymns. Anyone who tired of sitting and listening to the singing could walk out into the churchyard to visit with friends and neighbors.

The night before the "singing," a pit would have been dug on the edge of the grounds and a big pig would have roasted all night so that when the contents of the picnic baskets were brought out for the "dinner on the ground," there was plenty of delicious barbecue for all the crowd.

HERB ROAST CHICKEN
WITH CORNBREAD DRESSING

roasting chicken
salt and freshly ground pepper
sage, fresh or dried

HEARTH METHOD: Rub chicken with salt, pepper, and sage. Attach chicken to spit, place in reflector oven, and set oven before a brisk fire. Roast for about two hours or until bird is nicely browned and tests done. Baste with the drippings as necessary.

MODERN METHOD: Place prepared chicken in roasting pan. Place pan in preheated 350° oven and roast until the bird is nicely browned and tests done. Baste with drippings as necessary.

NOTE: Chicken is done when the leg and wing joints can be easily moved. Juices should run clear if chicken is pricked with a fork.

CORNBREAD DRESSING

1/2 cup butter
1 cup chopped celery
3/4 cup chopped onion
6 cups crumbled, stale corn bread
4 cups crumbled, stale biscuits
2 teaspoons salt
1/2 teaspoon freshly ground pepper
4 eggs, beaten
4 cups homemade chicken broth
1/2 teaspoon sage

HEARTH METHOD: Melt butter in spider placed over coals on hearth. Add and saute the celery and onion until soft but not brown. Add remainder of the ingredients to make moist dressing. The dressing should be very moist to ensure that the finished product will not be dry. Put dressing in greased baking pan. Set pan in preheated Dutch oven and bake for about 30 minutes, until brown but still moist.

MODERN METHOD: Saute vegetables in melted butter over low heat. Bake dressing in preheated 350° oven for about 30 minutes, until brown and still moist.

SOUTHERN FRIED CHICKEN

If you carefully follow these directions, your Southern fried chicken will be cooked to the bone, brown, crisp, and delicious.

large frying chicken
flour
salt and freshly ground pepper
1/2 cup lard

Mix flour, salt, and pepper. Roll chicken in mixture until well coated.

HEARTH METHOD: In a skillet or spider placed over coals on hearth, melt enough lard, about 1/2 inch, to fry chicken. When lard is hot, put the largest pieces of chicken in the middle of the pan and the smaller toward the edge. Cook over high heat until well-browned, turning only once.

When chicken is brown, lower heat by raking away some of the coals or letting burn down. Cover the pan tightly. Cook for 10 minutes, remove lid, turn chicken, recover, and cook for an additional 10 minutes.

At this time, add more coals; remove lid allowing the chicken to crisp, turning as necessary. Remove browned chicken and drain.

MODERN METHOD: Brown the chicken, as in hearth method, over high heat. Cook chicken by covering the skillet and lowering the fire. Uncover the skillet, raise heat, and brown and turn until brown and crisp.

ROAST CHRISTMAS GOOSE WITH FILLING

What could be more traditional than roasting a goose for Christmas? Or more delicious?

1 pound potatoes, peeled and cubed
water to cover

goose neck and giblets
water to cover
1/2 teaspoon salt
1/4 teaspoon pepper, freshly ground

1/2 cup butter
1 1/2 cups finely chopped onions
1/2 cup parsley, finely chopped
1/2 cup celery, finely chopped
1 teaspoon thyme
3/4 teaspoon marjoram
1/2 teaspoon rubbed sage
1 cup fine bread crumbs (from homemade bread)
1 10-pound goose
needle and cotton thread for sewing goose shut
flour, about 1/4 cup
lard, about 2 tablespoons

HEARTH METHOD: Mashed Potatoes: Put 1 pound of peeled, cubed potatoes in pot, cover with water, and hang pot on crane over brisk fire. When potatoes are done, drain and mash.

Goose Neck and Giblets: Cook the goose neck and giblets by putting in pot, covering with water and seasoning with salt and pepper. Cover the pot and hang from crane over brisk fire, cooking until done, about 30 minutes. Remove cooked meat from broth, cool, and chop finely.

Filling: Melt butter in spider over heap of coals on hearth. Add onions, celery, parsley, thyme, marjoram, sage. Cook, stirring, until the vegetables are done. Add the bread crumbs and the mashed potatoes and allow to cook for a few minutes. If the filling is too dry, add some of the broth in which the neck and giblets were cooked. Test and, if necessary, add salt and pepper. Allow the filling to cool.

Fill the goose and sew the opening. Spit the goose and dust lightly with flour. Place spit in reflector oven and roast, turning and basting with lard as necessary. Cook for about two hours or until goose tests done, when legs move easily and juices run clear.

MODERN METHOD: Prepare the potatoes as in hearth method over moderate heat.

Cook the goose neck and giblets as in hearth method, cooking over moderate heat until done.

Prepare the filling as in hearth method in skillet over moderate heat. Cool the filling, stuff the goose, sew, then place in baking pan. Dust with flour. Roast the stuffed goose in a 400° oven for about two hours or until it tests done.

GRAVY

drippings from goose
1 cup boiling water
butter
flour
salt and freshly ground pepper

HEARTH METHOD: Drain the drippings from the reflector oven. Add sufficient boiling water to drippings and cook for a few minutes. Combine the butter with flour and stir into mixture, stirring until thickened. Season with salt and freshly ground pepper.

MODERN METHOD: Prepare as in hearth method, cooking in skillet over low heat.

DEVILED CRAB

Mustard, that favorite herb of early English cooking, gives this dish the "heat" reflected in the name. Near the shore, the mixture is baked in well-scrubbed crab shells.

2 cups fresh bread crumbs from homemade bread
1 1/2 cups rich milk
1/2 teaspoon ground mustard
1 teaspoon salt
1/2 teaspoon ground red pepper
1 pound crab meat
1 beaten egg
2 tablespoons butter, melted

HEARTH METHOD: Soak 1 cup of the bread crumbs in the milk. Add seasonings, crab meat, egg, and then the melted butter. Fill crab shells, or buttered pudding dish. Cover with remaining cup of buttered crumbs. Bake in preheated Dutch oven for about 45 minutes or until done and browned.

MODERN METHOD: Follow hearth method, baking in preheated 350° oven about 35 minutes or until done and nicely browned.

MRS. HOWARD'S CRAB OLIO

This unusual and delicious crab recipe is from *Fifty Years in a Maryland Kitchen* by Mrs. B. C. Howard, published in 1873. Mrs. Howard was a popular Baltimore hostess of the 19th century.

1 large eggplant, peeled and sliced
6 large tomatoes
1 pound crab meat
3 eggs, beaten
salt and freshly ground pepper
1 cup buttered bread crumbs, homemade

HEARTH METHOD: Cook the eggplant in small amount of water over low flame until done. Dip tomatoes in boiling water for about one minute until peels will slip off easily. Add crab meat, eggs, seasonings, and breadcrumbs. Put in pudding pan, top with buttered crumbs, and place in preheated Dutch oven. Bake for about 30 minutes until done and nicely browned.

MODERN METHOD: Cook eggplant over low heat. Scald tomatoes and peel. Prepare mixture as in hearth method. Put in buttered ovenproof dish and bake in preheated 350° oven for 30 minutes or until done and browned.

FRIED RIVER FISH

For maximum flavor, fish should be cooked as soon as possible after being caught. This is the reason a riverside fish fry is so popular.

lard
1/2 cup corn meal
1 teaspoon salt
large mess of fish

HEARTH METHOD: Heat lard (enough to deep fry) in large pot over brisk fire. Mix meal and salt. Roll the fish in mixture until well coated. When lard is smoking hot, drop fish into pot and cook until golden brown and done.

MODERN METHOD: Heat lard in large frying pan over high heat. Follow hearth method for cooking.

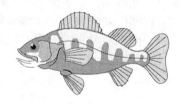

FRIED OYSTERS BALTIMORE

For many years, the Chesapeake Bay yielded a bountiful harvest of oysters. Raw bars abounded in old Baltimore and the low cost of oysters made them available to all. Today, because of overharvesting and pollution of the bay, the watermen's catch continues to decrease, resulting in higher prices. Oyster suppers are, however, still social events as well as the means whereby money is raised by clubs and churches.

1 egg, beaten
large, freshly shucked oysters, drained
bread crumbs, finely grated
1/2 teaspoon salt
1/4 teaspoon ground red pepper
lard, sufficient to fry

HEARTH METHOD: Beat the egg slightly, dip oysters in egg and then roll in the bread crumbs to which the seasonings have been added. Allow oyster coating to set for a few minutes. Set spider over hot coals and heat the lard. Fry oysters until nicely browned. Drain and serve at once.

MODERN METHOD: Follow hearth method to prepare oysters. Fry oysters in frying pan over high heat until done and brown.

COLONIST'S OYSTER PYE

The secret for making oyster "pye" is to avoid overcooking the oysters. This is accomplished by preparing the crust and filling separately and combining them shortly before serving.

pastry, sufficient to line pan and for top crust (recipe page 122)
1 quart oysters
3 tablespoons butter
1 medium onion, finely chopped
2 stalks celery, finely chopped
3 tablespoons flour
1/4 teaspoon nutmeg, freshly grated
1/2 teaspoon mace
1/4 teaspoon pepper, freshly ground
1/4 teaspoon red pepper, ground
1 cup heavy cream

HEARTH METHOD: Prepare pastry according to directions. Pinch off a small portion of dough and roll it into a circle the diameter of the pudding pan in which the pye will bake. Place the circle of pastry in a baking pan and bake in a preheated Dutch oven until nicely browned, about 15 minutes. Set aside. Roll out the remainder of the pastry and line the pudding pan. Place the pan in a preheated Dutch oven and bake for about 20 minutes until done and brown. Set aside.

Drain the liquid from the oysters. Melt the butter in spider set over small amount of coals placed on hearth. Add the chopped onions and celery and cook, stirring until soft. Stir in flour and the seasonings. Add the oyster liquor. Let the flavors mingle for a few minutes, being careful that it does not stick or burn. Add the cream gradually and when hot, add the oysters. Allow to cook gently for about five minutes until oysters are heated through and have begun to curl. Fill the baked crust with the filling, put on the top and serve immediately.

MODERN METHOD: Follow hearth directions for preparing pastry. Bake in preheated 450° oven for about 12-15 minutes.

Prepare the pie filling as in hearth method, cooking over moderate heat.

Fill the baked crust with the prepared filling, put on the baked top and serve immediately.

Part Three:
Fruits, Vegetables,
and Side Dishes

ROASTED APPLES

Roasted or baked apples make a simple delicious dessert, made elegant by the addition of rich, thick cream. Try serving baked apples for breakfast.

cooking apples, one for each person
1/4 cup butter
1/4 cup sugar
1/2 teaspoon cinnamon

Partially core apples in order to hold seasoning mixture. Put small amount of butter, sugar and cinnamon in each apple.

HEARTH METHOD: If using apple roaster, arrange apples on shelves and set the roaster in front of the fire. When the apples have browned, turn them and brown the other side. The juices will collect on the shelf of the roaster and can be spooned over the apples.

When baking the apples in the Dutch oven, arrange in pie pan. Add 1/4 cup water. Set the pan in the preheated oven, cover, and place oven over bed of coals. Pile coals on the lid. Bake for about 30 minutes or until done.

MODERN METHOD: Preheat oven to 350°. Put apples in pie pan and place in oven. Bake for about 30 minutes or until done.

FRESH BUTTER BEANS OR LIMA BEANS

The butter bean, a distinctly Southern bean, is different from the Lima bean, being less coarse and often quite colorful. We sometimes lay whole pods of okra on top of the beans for the last fifteen minutes of cooking time, allowing the vegetables to cross flavor. Some prefer to cook butter beans with butter rather than meat and when done to add a small amount of cream.

3 pounds of fresh beans
water to cover
2 slices bacon or thinly sliced salt pork
1/2 teaspoon salt

Shell and pick over the beans, then wash in cool water.

HEARTH METHOD: Put beans in pot and cover with cold water. Add meat and salt if using bacon; salt pork may provide enough salt to season. Cover pot and hang on crane over moderate flames. Bring beans to boil and then move pot away from center to simmer for about 30 minutes or until soft and done.

MODERN METHOD: Prepare beans as in hearth method. Bring to boil over high heat then lower heat to simmer beans until soft and done.

FRESH SNAP BEANS WITH BACON

A long, slow cooking period (sometimes several hours) is required to bring out the true, wonderful flavor of fresh snap beans. The modern method is to cook for only a few minutes to retain color and crispness but the flavor does not develop completely.

3 pounds string or snap beans, fresh
water to cover
strip salt pork or 2 slices bacon, diced
1/2 teaspoon salt

Remove the tips from beans and cut or snap into one-inch pieces. Wash several times in cold water.

HEARTH METHOD: Place beans, meat, salt (may not be necessary if using salt pork) and water to cover in pot. Place lid on pot and hang on crane over brisk flames. Bring to boil and then move to end of crane to allow to simmer for one hour or until completely done. If more water is needed, add boiling water.

MODERN METHOD: Prepare beans as in hearth method. Bring to boil over high heat and then lower heat to simmer beans for one hour or until done.

HOT BUTTERED BEETS

Hot buttered beets were served for summer meals. Pickled beets were prepared to bring not only delicious flavor but their rich color to drab winter meals.

3 pounds fresh beets
water to cover
1/2 teaspoon salt
1/4 teaspoon pepper, freshly ground
2 tablespoons butter

For maximum flavor, always select beets of small or medium size as the large ones are tough and lack the pleasant, sweet taste of the smaller ones. Cut off the beet tops but leave a short stem (which prevents the beet from "bleeding," or losing its juice). Wash beets in several changes of water.

HEARTH METHOD: Place beets in large pot, add water to cover. Hang pot over brisk fire and cook from one to two hours, depending on the size of the beets. Add boiling water as needed during cooking time. When the beets are done, remove from water and allow to become cool enough to handle. Slip off the peelings, the stem, and the root. Slice the beets (which should still be hot inside), butter, and sprinkle with salt and pepper.

MODERN METHOD: Prepare beets as in hearth method. Cook over medium heat.

CREAMED CABBAGE

Cabbage seeds were among those brought by colonists when they came to the New World. Cabbage had long been a favorite vegetable because of its "keeping" quality as well as its many uses. New cabbage is best for this recipe.

1 large new cabbage
3 tablespoons butter
1 tablespoon flour
salt and freshly ground pepper
1/2 cup heavy cream

Prepare fresh, new cabbage by removing the outer leaves and stalk and coarsely chopping.

HEARTH METHOD: Put cabbage in pot, cover with cold water. Hang pot over brisk flames and when cabbage boils, move the pot to the end of the spit to simmer. Cook until the cabbage is barely tender but not soft, about 15 minutes. Drain cabbage well and keep warm.

In spider over coals, melt the butter then mix in flour, salt and pepper. Stirring constantly, add cream and mix well, cooking until mixture has thickened. Add the cooked, drained cabbage, cover and cook until hot and the flavors have blended.

MODERN METHOD: Prepare cabbage as in hearth method, cooking cabbage over low heat.

COLCANNON

This dish, which combines those two favorites, potatoes and cabbage, was popular in both Scotland and Ireland. It was brought to America where it is usually served on St. Patrick's Day. It is delicious with cold meat.

2 pounds boiled and mashed potatoes
1 large cabbage, chopped and boiled until just tender
salt and freshly ground pepper
2 leeks, cooked and mashed
3 tablespoons butter
1/2 cup heavy cream

Wash, peel, and dice the potatoes.

Remove outer leaves from cabbage. Wash, quarter and remove stalk. Chop coarsely.

Split leeks and wash in several changes of water to insure that all sand is removed. Chop the leeks, including a small portion of the green part.

HEARTH METHOD: Place the potatoes in pot, cover with water, and add salt. Cover pot and hang from crane to cook over brisk fire until done, about 15 minutes. Drain the potatoes and mash.

Cook chopped leeks in a pot with a small amount of water placed over coals on hearth. When the leeks are tender and done, after about 10 minutes, drain and mash.

Mix the three prepared vegetables, add butter, cream and additional seasonings. Stir over low heat until the butter has melted and the vegetables are mixed. Serve very hot.

MODERN METHOD: Prepare the vegetables and cook each separate vegetable as in hearth method, cooking over low heat.

Combine the vegetables and heat over low heat, following hearth method.

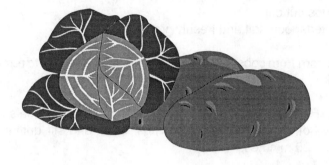

GREEN FRIED CORN

Green corn should be cooked as soon as possible after being removed from stalks, as the sugar quickly turns to starch.

3 tablespoons bacon drippings or butter
3 cups cut corn
1/2 teaspoon salt and freshly ground pepper

Cut corn from cobs, run back of knife blade down cob to remove milk.

HEARTH METHOD: Heat drippings in spider over coals until very hot; add corn and seasonings. Cook and stir until thick, about 20 minutes.

MODERN METHOD: Follow hearth method, cooking corn over moderate heat.

GRITS

Grits, which is coarsely ground, dried hominy, has long been a favorite dish in the South and is delicious when served with gravy or a lot of butter. Grits can be served at breakfast, dinner, or supper.

5 cups water
1 cup grits
1/2 teaspoon salt
2 tablespoons butter
1/4 teaspoon pepper, freshly ground

HEARTH METHOD: Bring water to boil in iron pot hung from crane over brisk fire. Stir grits and salt into briskly boiling water. Cover pot and move to end of the crane away from the center of the fire. Cook for 15-20 minutes or until thickened, stirring occasionally. Remove from fire. Stir well; add butter and freshly ground pepper.

MODERN METHOD: Bring water to boil over high heat. Stir in the grits and salt, cover pot, lower heat. Cook for 15-20 minutes or until thickened, stirring occasionally.

CHURCH SUPPER CORN PUDDING

Church suppers, though held in the church, were sometimes purely social gatherings, a chance for friends and relatives to come together to share food and good times. Each family brought a dish which was put on the table to be shared by all. This was another occasion for the cooks of the community to bring the dish for which they were best known. These suppers were sometimes preceded or followed by a worship service.

Corn pudding, many cooks' specialty, has a firm, custard-like consistency which makes it easy to transport to the church supper where it is a much sought-after favorite. Farm wives usually had most of the required ingredients on hand—corn, milk, butter, and eggs.

3 cups cut corn
2 tablespoons flour
1 tablespoon sugar
1/2 teaspoon salt
1/4 teaspoon pepper, freshly ground
pinch red pepper, ground
1 1/2 cups milk
3 eggs, slightly beaten
2 tablespoons butter, melted

Cut corn from cobs, run back of knife blade down cobs to remove milk. Add flour, sugar, salt and peppers to corn. Stir in milk, eggs and melted butter. Mix well.

HEARTH METHOD: Pour into buttered pudding pan. Place pan in preheated Dutch oven. Bake for about 45 minutes. The pudding is done when knife inserted in center comes out clean.

MODERN METHOD: Follow hearth method, baking pudding in ovenproof dish in preheated 350° oven. Bake for about 45 minutes, testing as in hearth method.

GREENS: TURNIP, MUSTARD, COLLARD, KALE

Turnip greens are the favorite greens of the South where it is possible to grow two crops each year, one in the spring and one in the fall. Sometimes turnip greens are mixed with an equal amount of mustard greens. Cooking them together results in a different and delicious flavor. Collards are the favorite winter greens, reaching their true flavor only after a good frost. When greens are cooked with salt pork, the liquid resulting is a tasty broth known as "pot liquor." Pot liquor is served with hot cornbread as a soup meal.

large mess greens, about 2-3 pounds
2 teaspoons salt
1 pod hot red pepper
salt pork, 1/4 pound, diced (or ham hock or ham trimmings)
water, about one cup

Pick over greens carefully, removing any discolored leaves. Wash several times in cool water to remove all sand and grit.

HEARTH METHOD: Place the greens in large pot, add water, salt, pepper and the diced meat. Cover the pot and hang from crane over brisk fire. Bring to boil. Move pot to end of spit and cook slowly until done, about one hour. Remove from heat, drain off, and save the pot liquor. Cut up the greens for easy serving. Serve with diced meat on top of the greens.

MODERN METHOD: Follow hearth method. Bring to boil over high heat then lower heat, simmering the greens for about one hour or until done.

GREEN GARDEN PEAS

In the South of my childhood, these peas were referred to as "English" peas. Because the season for them was so short, they were considered a special treat.

3 pounds green peas
1 cup water
1/2 teaspoon salt
2 tablespoons butter

Select peas with well-filled pods, shell and wash carefully.

HEARTH METHOD: Place peas in pot and add small amount of water. Hang pot over brisk fire, bring to boil. Simmer peas away from direct flame for about 10-15 minutes until just tender. Add salt and butter. If you prefer the liquid to be sightly thickened, rub butter in one tablespoon flour and stir into liquid. A small amount of cream will improve the flavor.

MODERN METHOD: Prepare peas as in hearth method; bring to boil over high heat. Reduce heat and simmer gently until peas are soft.

BLACK-EYED PEAS

The favorite and best known of all the types of peas which are grown in the South, black-eyed peas are especially delicious when slow-cooked at the hearth. Be sure to serve with hot cornbread and pepper sauce.

2 cups dried black-eyed peas
1 quart water
1 teaspoon salt
1 pod red pepper
1/4 pound salt pork, diced
1 medium onion, diced

Pick over the peas, wash in cold water. Soak the peas overnight in cold water.

HEARTH METHOD: Place the peas, with the water in which they were soaked, in iron pot. Add salt, pepper, salt pork, and onion. Cover and bring to boil over brisk flame. Move pot away from flame and allow to simmer until done, about one hour.

MODERN METHOD: Follow hearth method for preparing peas. Bring to boil over high heat then reduce heat and simmer the peas until tender, about one hour.

"GRABBLED" NEW POTATOES

As soon as my mother felt that the Irish potatoes had grown to eating size, she would take a large cooking fork and head for the garden. She would carefully dig beneath each potato plant and with her hand she would "grabble" for the potatoes, removing from the roots any that were big enough for cooking.

mess new potatoes, about 3 pounds
1/2 teaspoon salt
water
2 tablespoons butter, melted

Wash and carefully scrub the potatoes but do not peel them.

HEARTH METHOD: Place potatoes in pot, and add salt and enough cold water to cover. Hang pot over flames and bring to a boil. Continue cooking for about 25 minutes or until the potatoes test done. Drain well and place in serving bowl. Set bowl in warm place.

In a spider placed over the coals on hearth, melt the butter. Pour the melted butter over the potatoes and serve while quite hot.

MODERN METHOD: Prepare the potatoes as in hearth method. Cook over medium heat until the potatoes test done.

CANDIED SWEET POTATOES

Sweet potatoes are among the crops for which Maryland's Eastern Shore is well-known. The shore's sandy soil is ideal because good drainage is essential for the growing of sweet potatoes. The sweet potato, Ipomsea batatas, is not to be confused with the true yam which is grown only in the southernmost part of the United States. The yam is sweeter and of a deeper orange color. Both the sweet potato and the yam can be prepared in a variety of ways, from french fries to delicious pie.

6 medium-sized sweet potatoes, all the same size
water to cover
1/3 cup butter
2/3 cup brown sugar
1/2 teaspoon salt
1/3 cup water

Wash and scrub potatoes thoroughly.

HEARTH METHOD: Place potatoes in pot and cover with water. Hang the pot over flames until potatoes are half-done. Remove the potatoes from pot, peel and slice about one inch thick. Melt butter in spider placed over coals on hearth. Add brown sugar and cook, stirring, until blended. Add the potato slices, cook, turning until well-coated and brown. Add salt and water cover, and continue to cook until the potatoes are tender.

MODERN METHOD: Follow hearth method for cooking the potatoes in a pot over medium heat. Finish cooking in skillet over medium heat.

DUTCH OVEN ROASTED SWEET POTATOES

4 potatoes, uniform size
2 tablespoons lard or bacon grease

Wash, scrub, and then dry potatoes. Rub potatoes with a small amount of lard or bacon grease.

HEARTH METHOD: Place potatoes in preheated Dutch oven set over coals and bake for about one hour or until potatoes feel soft when gently squeezed.

MODERN METHOD: Bake the potatoes as in hearth method, placing in 350° preheated oven.

POTATO PUFFS

With the big meal, dinner, being served midday, sometimes there were not enough leftovers for supper. It was then that the housewife would prepare a dish such as potato puffs to "fill out" the meal.

2 cups mashed potatoes (hot or leftover)
1/4 cup flour
1 1/2 teaspoons baking powder
1/2 teaspoon salt
1 egg
1 onion, small, finely diced or 1 tablespoon
    chives, finely chopped
2 tablespoons butter

If using fresh potatoes, wash, peel, and dice.

HEARTH METHOD: Place potatoes in pot, cover with cold water. Hang pot on crane over fire and boil until the potatoes are done, about 15 minutes. Remove from heat, drain, and mash.

Mix flour, baking powder and salt and add to mashed potatoes. Add beaten egg and onion or chives, mix well. Melt butter in spider placed over hot coals on hearth. Drop potato mixture by the tablespoonfuls to form small cakes. Cook until nicely browned; turn and brown on the other side.

MODERN METHOD: Prepare potatoes as in hearth method, cooking over moderate heat.

Follow the hearth method for mixing puffs and cook over moderate heat.

RICE

Early in its history, South Carolina was well-known for the production of rice. Rice became a popular dish not only there but throughout the South, which is still among the world leaders in rice production.

1 cup rice
2 1/2 cups water
1 teaspoon salt
1 tablespoon butter

HEARTH METHOD: Bring water to boil in pot hung over low fire. Add rice, salt, and butter, cover pot tightly, and simmer for 20 minutes, then lightly stir with fork.

MODERN METHOD: Follow hearth method, simmering rice over low heat.

SUMMER SQUASH CAKES

These squash cakes, distinctive by the inclusion of chives, are popular with participants of the hearth cooking workshops which I teach at the museum.

2 cups squash, coarsely grated
1/2 teaspoon salt
1/4 teaspoon pepper, freshly ground
1/2 tablespoon chives, chopped
1 egg, slightly beaten
1/2 teaspoon baking powder
1/2 cup flour
2 tablespoons bacon grease

HEARTH METHOD: Wash squash carefully and coarsely grate. Add salt, pepper, chives, and egg. Mix well. Mixture should be juicy. Combine baking powder with flour and add enough to squash mixture to obtain consistency necessary for dropping by tablespoonfuls into hot bacon grease heated in spider over hot coals.

MODERN METHOD: Make cake mixture as in hearth method, cooking in frying pan over high heat.

Part Four: Bread

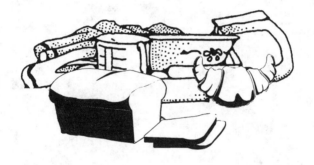

BUTTERMILK BISCUITS

The gentlemen's favorite!

2 cups flour
2 teaspoons baking powder
1/2 teaspoon baking soda
1/2 teaspoon salt
1/3 cup lard
1 cup buttermilk
2 tablespoons lard

Combine flour, baking powder, baking soda, and salt. Cut in the lard and lightly mix with a fork. Gradually add the buttermilk stirring with fork just until blended. Turn onto floured board and knead gently six times. Pat or roll to 1/2" thickness. Cut into rounds.

Melt the 2 tablespoons lard in iron biscuit pan. Turn each biscuit in the melted lard, then arrange in pan. Allow biscuits to touch each other if soft sides are desired.

HEARTH METHOD: Place pan in preheated Dutch oven and bake for about 15 minutes or until done and nicely browned, top and bottom.

To bake in biscuit oven, place biscuits on oven shelf. Set oven before fire and bake for about 12-15 minutes.

MODERN METHOD: Follow hearth method, baking in preheated 450° oven for 12-15 minutes.

Rosemary, chives, marjoram, parsley, or sage can be added with the dry ingredients to make lovely herb biscuits. They are delightful served for tea when cut with a small round cutter.

MARYLAND BEATEN BISCUITS

This is an interesting recipe although it requires more time and labor than we are now accustomed to devoting to "quick" bread. The beating lightens the dough and no leavening is used. Follow directions exactly.

5 cups flour
1/2 tablespoon salt
2 tablespoons lard
water

Add salt to flour, mix, then cut in lard. Add enough cool water to make a stiff dough. Place the mixed dough on a firm surface (a tree stump was the choice in early Maryland). Beat the dough with the flat of an axe, folding and beating until the dough blisters and pops. When it is satin smooth, pinch off dough in golf-ball-sized pieces, flatten slightly and prick top with a fork. Place biscuits in greased pan; do not allow to touch each other.

HEARTH METHOD: Bake in preheated Dutch oven for 20-30 minutes until done and slightly browned.

To bake in biscuit oven, place biscuits on oven shelf. Set oven before fire and bake for about 20-30 minutes.

MODERN METHOD: Follow the hearth method, baking in preheated 450° oven for 20-30 minutes.

The biscuits are elegant when served with very thin slices of Maryland ham.

CORNBREAD

It was cornbread which could be considered the staff of life for early settlers in America. After the Indians taught them how to grow maize, the colonists soon developed their own method for making a tasty bread from the ground grain. Corn bread was, and is, a very versatile bread which can be served at breakfast, dinner and supper as well as for snacks. It is also used as the base for other dishes such as dressing.

2 tablespoons shortening
1 cup white corn meal
1/2 cup flour
1 teaspoon baking powder
1/2 teaspoon salt
1/2 teaspoon baking soda
1 egg
1 cup buttermilk

HEARTH METHOD: Preheat Dutch oven and set over a pile of coals on the hearth. Put shortening in iron bread pan and place in Dutch oven to heat. Mix cornmeal, flour, baking powder, salt, and baking soda. Add egg and buttermilk. Stir well. Add the heated shortening, mix and pour corn bread mixture into the heated pan. Set pan in Dutch oven, cover and pile coals on lid. Bake for about 20 minutes or until done and brown.

MODERN METHOD: Follow hearth method for preparing mix. Heat shortening in 450° oven. Add hot shortening to mix, stir, pour into hot bread pan and bake about 20 minutes or until done.

For a delightfully different taste, add one tablespoon of a favorite herb to the cornbread. Mince the herb finely. Among herbs from which to choose are rosemary, chives, dill, oregano, or marjoram.

TEATIME CRUMPETS

Crumpets are fun to bake on the griddle to serve freshly cooked with butter, jam, and tea. These crumpets have the same interesting texture as English muffins. Crumpet rings can easily be made by removing the bottoms of small tuna cans.

4 1/2 cups flour	2 cups milk
1 tablespoon yeast	1 teaspoon salt

HEARTH METHOD: Heat the milk until tepid in a saucepan placed on a trivet over a small pile of coals on hearth. Remove from heat.

Dissolve the yeast in a small amount of the warm milk. Put the flour and salt into a bowl and stir together. Make a well in the dry mixture and pour in the yeast and remaining milk, stir well with a wooden spoon. Cover the bowl and place in a warm place to rise.

HEARTH METHOD: Lightly grease a griddle and place the greased crumpet rings on it. (If your kitchen is not equipped with a hanging griddle, cook the crumpets in an iron frying pan placed on a trivet over a pile of coals on hearth.) Spoon in enough of the crumpet mixture to half fill the rings. Hang griddle over fire and bake until bubbles form on the top and the bottoms have browned. Remove the rings, turn the crumpets over to brown the top side.

MODERN METHOD: Lightly grease a griddle or frying pan and place the greased crumpet rings on it. Half fill the crumpet rings. Place griddle or frying pan over moderate heat and bake as in hearth method.

Crumpets can be baked without the rings but will not be as high.

IRISH SODA BREAD

This bread is too good to bake only for St. Patrick's Day!

3 cups flour
2 tablespoons brown sugar
2 teaspoons baking powder
1 teaspoon baking soda
1 teaspoon salt
1/2 cup currants or raisins
2 teaspoons caraway seeds
1 1/2 cup buttermilk

Stir together the flour, brown sugar, baking powder, baking soda and the salt. Add the currants (or raisins) and the caraway seeds. Add buttermilk and stir until the dry ingredients are moistened. Turn onto a floured board and knead just to smooth and shape into a ball. Place in a greased, round pan. With a sharp knife, slash a deep X on the top of the loaf.

HEARTH METHOD: Place pan in preheated Dutch oven. Put the oven over coals on the hearth and put coals on the lid. Bake for about 40 minutes or until done and brown. Cool the bread for about 10 minutes in pan. Remove from the pan and cool thoroughly before slicing.

MODERN METHOD: Follow hearth method, baking in preheated 350° oven for about 40 minutes or until done and brown.

LIGHT BREAD

Yeast breads were never as popular in the South as were other types because the proper kinds of wheat would not grow there. This meant that until there were reliable means of transportation, the cooks relied on cornmeal. When our mother made "light bread," it was considered a real treat.

6 cups flour
1 package active dry yeast
2 1/4 cups milk
2 tablespoons sugar
1 tablespoon shortening
2 teaspoons salt

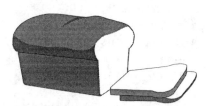

Mix 2 1/2 cups flour and the yeast. Heat until warm—but do not boil—2 1/2 cups milk, 2 tablespoons sugar, 1 tablespoon shortening, and salt. Add to the flour mixture. With a wooden spoon, beat in additional flour to make a stiff dough. Turn the dough out on a lightly floured board and knead for about 8-10 minutes, until smooth and elastic. Shape dough into ball and place in raised bowl. Turn dough, cover; let rise in warm place until doubled. Turn out on lightly floured board. Divide into two loaves; place in greased loaf pans. Cover and again let rise for about one hour or until again doubled.

HEARTH METHOD: Place the pans in heated Dutch oven set over coals on the hearth. Put coals on top of oven. Let the bread bake for about 45 minutes or until done and brown. Remove from pan and let cool.

MODERN METHOD: Follow hearth directions, baking bread in preheated 375° oven for about 45 minutes or until done.

MOTHER'S DINNER ROLLS

Dinner rolls were usually made for special occasions like Sunday dinner or when company came.

1 cup milk
1/4 cup sugar
4 tablespoons butter
1 teaspoon salt
1 package active dry yeast
2 tablespoons warm water
3 eggs
41/2 cups flour
2 tablespoons butter, melted

Heat milk to lukewarm, add sugar, butter, and salt. Let the mixture cool. Dissolve yeast in warm—not hot—water. Add the eggs to the cooled milk mixture, then add the yeast mixture. Add the flour gradually, mixing with a wooden spoon. Cover the dough and set in a warm place to rise.

After the dough has doubled in size, in about 2 hours, punch down. Knead dough slightly to smooth. Cut off a small amount of dough, roll to 1/2" thickness on floured board, and cut with a 2" biscuit cutter. Dip the cut rounds in the melted butter and place in pan. Let rise for one hour.

HEARTH METHOD: Bake the rolls in a preheated Dutch oven placed over coals on hearth. Place coals on lid. Bake for about 15-20 minutes until done and browned.

MODERN METHOD: Follow the hearth method for preparing the dough. Bake in preheated 400° oven for 15-20 minutes until the rolls are done.

CORNMEAL PONE

Pone is a cornbread made without eggs or milk unlike hush puppies. They are fried in only a small amount of grease and do not contain onion. These pones are especially popular for serving with turnip greens. This mixture is sometimes referred to as hot-water bread.

2 cups cornmeal
1/2 teaspoon salt
sufficient hot water to mix
lard

Add the salt to the cornmeal. Using a wooden spoon, stir in the hot water. Let the mixture stand for a few minutes. Add more hot water if necessary, but the dough must be stiff enough to hold its shape.

Shape pones about as large as an egg.

HEARTH METHOD: Melt sufficient lard to fry, about one-half inch, in spider over hot coals on hearth. Drop the pones into the hot lard and fry, turning once, until nicely browned and done. Be certain that the center of the pone is cooked. Remove and drain. Serve while hot.

MODERN METHOD: Follow the hearth method for preparing the pone mixture. Heat the lard in frying pan over high heat; cook until brown and done.

SALLY LUNN

Because Sally Lunn bread is considered so special, it is thought that it is difficult to make. It is really quite simple, requiring no kneading. We usually associate Sally Lunn with a visit to Williamsburg, but there is no reason why it can't be served at home. Sally Lunn is delicious whether served at breakfast, dinner, supper, or teatime.

1 package yeast
1/4 cup warm water
1 3/4 cups milk
2 tablespoons sugar
4 tablespoons butter
1 teaspoon salt
5 cups flour, approximately
2 eggs, well beaten

Dissolve the yeast in warm water. Heat the milk until almost boiling and pour over the sugar, butter, and salt in a mixing bowl. Cool the mixture. Sift the flour and beat the eggs. When the mixture has cooled, stir in the yeast, eggs, and 3 cups of the flour. Add enough additional flour to make a soft dough. Cover the dough and let rise in a warm place until doubled in bulk, about one hour.

Beat the dough down and place in a buttered tube pan or 2 loaf pans. Let rise for about 30 minutes or until dough has increased in bulk by about one half.

HEARTH METHOD: Place pan in preheated Dutch oven. Set the oven on pile of coals on hearth and put coals on the lid. Bake for about 40 minutes or until done and brown.

MODERN METHOD: Heat oven to 350° and bake for 40 minutes, until the bread is done and brown.

SCONES ON THE GRIDDLE

Put on the teapot and get out the jam jar to serve with these hot, delicious scones.

1 1/2 teaspoons baking soda
1 1/2 teaspoons cream of tartar
1 teaspoon salt
1/4 cup sugar
3 cups flour
2/3 cup lard
1 1/2 cups buttermilk

Add baking soda, cream of tartar, salt, and sugar to the flour and mix well. Cut in 1/3 cup lard. Add the buttermilk and stir until just blended to form a soft dough. Turn the dough out onto a floured board and divide into 3 balls of equal size. Pat each ball into a circle 1/2" thick. Cut the circle into 4 triangles.

HEARTH METHOD: Heat griddle over blaze and grease with 1/3 cup of the additional lard. Brown each triangle on both sides, turning once.

MODERN METHOD: Follow the hearth method, baking the scones on heated greased griddle over high heat.

SOUTHERN SPOON BREAD

Spoon bread is a traditional bread in the South, another use for the corn introduced to the colonists by the Indians.

1 cup white cornmeal
2 cups boiling water
3 tablespoons butter
1 teaspoon salt
2 cups milk
3 eggs
2 teaspoons baking powder

HEARTH METHOD: Place meal in pot and over it pour 2 cups of boiling water as you stir. Set pan on trivet over coals on hearth and boil for five minutes, continuing to stir. Remove from coals; add butter, salt, and milk. Mix well. Beat eggs until light and add to mixture. Sift in the baking powder; stir thoroughly; pour into greased pudding dish. Place dish in preheated Dutch oven. Set the oven on coals on hearth and put coals on top. Bake for about 30 minutes.

MODERN METHOD: Prepare same as in hearth method. Bake in preheated 350° oven for about 30 minutes.

Spoon bread traditionally is served with the spoon from the dish in which it was baked.

Part Five: Dessert

APPLESAUCE CAKE

Although not native to America, the colonists quickly established orchards and made apples an important part of their diet. The cooks devised many ways to utilize this versatile fruit. One of its most appreciated attributes was that it could be dried for winter use, this at a time when methods of food preservation were limited.

2 teaspoons baking soda
1 1/2 cups applesauce, homemade, unsweetened
1 tablespoon cinnamon
1 1/2 teaspoons cloves, ground
1/2 teaspoon freshly grated nutmeg
1 1/2 cups sugar
21/2 cups flour
1/2 cup butter, melted
1 cup currants
1/2 cup nuts, chopped

Stir baking soda into applesauce and set aside. Mix the dry ingredients adding cinnamon, cloves, nutmeg, and sugar to the flour. Stir and mix, then add to the applesauce mixture. Stir in the melted butter, currants, and chopped nuts.

HEARTH METHOD: Pour mixed batter into a greased, floured cake pan. Place in preheated Dutch oven set on coals on the hearth. Pile coal on oven lid. Bake for 45 minutes, or until the cake tests done. Leave cake in for 10 minutes when baking is completed.

MODERN METHOD: Follow the hearth method for preparing cake batter. Pour into greased, floured tube pan and bake in preheated 350° oven for 45 minutes or until cake tests done.

ELECTION DAY CAKE

In New England, these cakes were prepared and eaten to celebrate an election victory or while awaiting the returns. The yeast gives the cake a bread-like texture and taste which is typical of cakes of that period before baking powder.

21/2 cups flour
1 package active dry yeast
1/4 teaspoon salt
1/4 teaspoon freshly ground nutmeg
1 cup milk
1/4 cup granulated sugar
1/4 cup packed brown sugar
1/4 cup butter
1 egg
1 cup currants or raisins

HEARTH METHOD: Combine of flour, yeast, salt, and nutmeg. In a spider over coals on the hearth, heat milk, granulated sugar, brown sugar and butter until warm, stirring constantly.

Add milk mixture to the dry mixture. Slightly beat, then add egg and currants or raisins. With a wooden spoon, beat the mixture for about 5 minutes. Cover, let rise in warm place until doubled, about 1-1 1/2 hours. Stir the dough down. Spoon onto a greased loaf pan and let rise again until doubled, about 1 hour. Bake in preheated Dutch oven; set on coals with coals piled on top for about 45 minutes, until the cake tests done.

MODERN METHOD: Follow the hearth method, heating the milk mixture in a small pan over moderate heat. Bake in preheated 350° oven about 45 minutes or until cake tests done.

GEORGE WASHINGTON'S FAVORITE CAKE

We cannot be sure this was Washington's favorite cake. We do know it is a favorite to bake at the hearth in a Dutch oven.

3/4 cup butter
1 1/2 cups sugar
3 eggs
1/4 cup red wine
1 teaspoon baking soda
2 teaspoons freshly grated nutmeg
1 1/2 teaspoons cinnamon
3 cups flour
1 cup heavy cream

HEARTH METHOD: Beat the eggs, add wine and then combine with the butter and sugar mixture. Cream the butter until light and fluffy. Add the sugar, a small amount at a time, beating after each addition. Beat the eggs, add wine, and then combine with the butter and sugar mixture.

Mix the baking soda and spices with the flour. Add one third of the flour mixture to the butter and egg mixture. Add half of the heavy cream. Add the second third of the flour mixture, the remaining half of the cream and then the remainder of the flour.

Put batter into two greased pie plates and bake in preheated Dutch oven for about 30 minutes or until it tests done.

MODERN METHOD: Mix cake batter as for hearth method. Bake in 350° oven until the cake tests done.

Serve the cooled cake in pie-slice wedges. A dab of whipped cream is a nice addition.

We usually bake this cake at our February hearth cooking workshop at which time we celebrate Washington's birthday.

LOAF GINGER BREAD

This is the treat sometimes called Muster Day Gingerbread that the men of the colonies looked forward to enjoying with rum after drills were finished.

1/3 cup lard
1 teaspoon baking soda
1/2 cup packed brown sugar
3/4 teaspoon ground ginger
1/2 cup dark molasses
3/4 teaspoon ground cinnamon
1 egg
1/4 teaspoon ground cloves
2 cups flour
1/2 cup boiling water

Cream lard and sugar together until fluffy. Mix molasses and egg together; add to sugar mixture. Mix dry ingredients and add to creamed mixture alternately with boiling water. Beat after each addition. Pour into greased and floured loaf pan.

HEARTH METHOD: Place loaf pan in preheated Dutch oven sat on bed of coals on hearth. Put coals on lid. Bake the gingerbread for about 50 minutes or until it tests done. Cool 10 minutes; remove from pan; cool thoroughly.

MODERN METHOD: Place loaf pan in preheated 350° oven and bake for 50 minutes or until cake tests done. Follow hearth method for removal and cooling.

This gingerbread should be wrapped and stored overnight before serving. Serve sliced gingerbread with ginger-flavored whipped cream.

ARKANSAS BLACKBERRY JAM CAKE

Homemade blackberry jam in Arkansas means jam cake. Each cook has her own special recipe for making this cake and this is the recipe which my mother used for her delicious cake.

5 eggs, separated
1 cup butter
2 cups sugar
1 1/2 cups blackberry jam
3 cups flour
1 teaspoon freshly grated nutmeg

1/2 teaspoon salt
1 teaspoon baking soda
1 cup butter milk
1 cup chopped pecans

Slightly beat the egg yolks. Beat the egg whites until stiff.

Cream butter and sugar; add slightly beaten egg yolks and the blackberry jam. Blend well. Mix flour, nutmeg, salt, and baking soda. Add to creamed mixture alternately with the buttermilk. Beat well. Fold in stiffly beaten egg whites and the chopped pecans. Pour into 3 buttered and floured 8" cake pans.

HEARTH METHOD: Put cake pan on trivet in preheated Dutch oven. Set the oven on pile of coals on hearth and pile coals on top. Bake about 30 minutes; test for doneness.

Cool cake for 10 minutes and then remove from pan. Cool thoroughly and then frost.

MODERN METHOD: Bake for 25 minutes in a preheated 350-degree oven.

FROSTING

3 cups sugar
1 1/2 cups milk
1/2 cup butter
1/2 cup heavy cream
1 teaspoon vanilla
1 cup chopped pecans

HEARTH METHOD: Bring sugar and milk to a boil in saucepan set on trivet over coals on hearth. Cook, stirring constantly, until mixture reaches soft ball stage. Remove from heat; stir in butter, cream, and vanilla. Beat until slightly thickened. Add the chopped nuts. Spread between cake layers and on top.

MODERN METHOD: Follow hearth method, cooking frosting over medium heat.

HOT MILK CAKE

Another old cake recipe, this one has been handed down from mother to daughter and is still popular with cooks because it is quick and easy to make and is delicious served plain.

4 eggs	2 teaspoons vanilla extract
2 cups sugar	3/4 cup melted butter
2 teaspoons baking powder	1 cup milk
2 cups flour	

Place the eggs in mixing bowl and beat well. Add the sugar one cup at a time, beating well after each addition. Add the baking powder to the flour, add gradually to egg mixture. Beat until the mixture is well mixed. Add vanilla and beat for one additional minute.

HEARTH METHOD: Melt the butter in small skillet over low coals. Put milk in saucepan; add melted butter and place on trivet over coals. Bring to boil. Remove from heat and add the egg mixture while the milk is very hot. Mix well and divide the batter between two greased and floured pans.

Place each pan in preheated Dutch oven. Set oven over coals and pile coals on top. Bake for about 25 minutes

MODERN METHOD: Follow the hearth method for preparing the batter. Melt the butter in small pan over low heat. Put milk in saucepan; add melted butter and bring milk to boil over medium heat. Remove pan from heat and add egg mixture while milk is very hot. Mix well and pour into 13" x 9" greased and floured pan. Bake for 25-30 minutes in preheated 350° oven or until cake tests done.

Powdered sugar can be sprinkled on top. If desired, serve with fresh fruit.

OLD-FASHIONED NUT LOAF

We had a large pecan tree in our backyard which furnished ample nuts for this and many other delicious recipes. Picking up the fallen pecans was one of my daily after-school chores.

1/2 cup butter
1 1/2 cups sugar
2 eggs
2 cups flour
1/4 teaspoon salt
1 teaspoon baking powder
3/4 cup water
1 teaspoon vanilla
1 cup pecans, halves or large pieces

Cream butter and sugar, add eggs. Sift flour, salt, and baking powder together. Add dry ingredients alternately with water to the butter mixture. Stir in vanilla and then beat until well-mixed. Add nuts and stir. Turn into greased and floured loaf pan.

HEARTH METHOD: Put pan on trivet in preheated Dutch oven. Set oven on coals on hearth and put coals on top. Bake for about 45 minutes or until the cake tests done.

MODERN METHOD: Bake the loaf in preheated 350° oven for about 45 minutes or until the cake tests done.

GLAZED PRUNE CAKE

Prunes, one of the few fruits available during the winter months, made this spice-type cake very popular. It was once advisable to soak the prunes overnight before using, but it is no longer necessary as they are now tenderized.

1/2 cup butter
1 1/2 cups sugar
3 eggs, beaten
2 cups flour
1 teaspoon baking soda
1/2 teaspoon salt
1 teaspoon cinnamon
1 teaspoon nutmeg, freshly grated
1 teaspoon ground cloves
1 cup buttermilk
1 teaspoon vanilla extract
1 cup chopped nuts
1 cup pitted, chopped prunes

Cream butter and sugar until fluffy. Add the eggs and mix well. Combine the dry ingredients and add alternately with the buttermilk to which the vanilla has been added. Add the nuts and chopped prunes; stir until well mixed.

HEARTH METHOD: Pour the batter into two square pans, well-buttered and floured. Place pans in preheated Dutch oven. Place oven over coals on hearth and put coals on top. Bake the cake for about 30 minutes or until cake tests done. Leave cake in pan.

MODERN METHOD: Prepare batter as in hearth method. Pour into a 9" x 19" pan, well-buttered and floured. Bake cake in preheated 325° oven for about 40 minutes or until the cake tests done. Leave cake in pan.

BUTTERMILK GLAZE

This glaze should be poured over cake while it is still hot.

1/2 cup buttermilk
1 cup sugar
1/2 teaspoon baking soda
1/2 cup butter
2 teaspoons vanilla

HEARTH METHOD: Combine all ingredients in saucepan. Set pan on trivet over pile of coals on hearth. Boil for one minute without beating.

MODERN METHOD: Combine all ingredients in saucepan. Boil over moderate heat for one minute. Do not beat.

RHUBARB CRUMBLE WITH CUSTARD

1 1/2 cups flour	1/2 cup sugar
1 1/2 cups dark brown sugar	2 tablespoons lemon juice
6 ounces butter, cut	1 pound rhubarb, washed,
in small pieces	cut 1" cubes

Preheat Dutch oven. Put the flour and brown sugar in a mixing bowl. Add the butter and rub it in with your fingers until the mixture resembles coarse bread crumbs.

Put the rhubarb in a pie or soufflé dish and sprinkle it with lemon juice, sugar, and cinnamon. Put mixture on top, pressing down gently; make sure that all the rhubarb is covered.

Bake in the oven for 20 minutes or until the crumble is golden and the rhubarb is beginning to bubble up around the edges. Serve hot or cold.

CUSTARD

1 1/2 cups flour	1/2 cup sugar
1 pound rhubarb, cut	6 ounces butter, cut in small
1" cube	pieces
1 1/2 cups dark brown sugar	2 tablespoons lemon juice

In heavy bottomed saucepan, mix 2 tablespoons of the milk with the cornstarch. As soon as the cornstarch is dissolved, add the rest of the milk and the sugar and cook over moderate heat until the sauce begins to thicken and comes to a boil.

Place the egg yolks in a bowl and beat them with a fork. Take a cup of the sauce and pour it over the eggs, beating as you pour. Return the mixture to the rest of the sauce, stir well and quickly bring it back to a boil. Add the lemon juice, remove from the heat. Pour into a pitcher and serve.

SHORTBREAD

I have often wished that I had the recipe for shortbread which my ancestors probably brought with them from Scotland. This is a real treat with an afternoon cup of tea.

1 cup butter
1/2 cup sugar
21/2 cups flour

Cream butter and gradually add sugar, creaming thoroughly. Beat the mixture until it is light and fluffy. Stir in the flour. Put the dough in a cool place for several hours. Divide the dough in half and pat each into circle to fit pan. With a fork, prick each circle to make wedges.

HEARTH METHOD: Place pan in preheated Dutch oven and set oven over coal. Put coals on top. Bake the shortbread for about 30 minutes until done and light brown. Cool the shortbread slightly before removing from the pan.

MODERN METHOD: Follow the hearth method for preparing the dough, baking in 300° oven for about 30 minutes until done and brown.

STRAWBERRY SHORTCAKE

Nothing is more simple, or more delicious, than a REAL strawberry shortcake!

21/2 cups flour
1 teaspoon salt
4 teaspoons baking powder
1 tablespoon sugar

1/3 cup milk
1 egg
3/4 cup milk

2 tablespoons butter
1 pint strawberries
1/2 pint cream whipped, slightly sweetened

Mix dry ingredients. Cut butter into the flour mixture. Put egg into milk and mix together. Add egg mixture to dry mixture and make into a dough. Turn on a floured board and knead until smooth.

Divide dough in two parts. Pat one part to fit a pie plate; sprinkle generously with flour. Roll out the second part and place on top.

HEARTH METHOD: Place pie plate in preheated Dutch oven. Put oven over coals on hearth and put coals on top. Bake the cake for about 30 minutes until well-done and lightly browned.

Separate the layers and spread generously with butter. Spread sliced, sweetened strawberries over the bottom layer; put on the top layer and spread more berries on top. Cover the top with whipped cream and decorate with several whole berries.

MODERN METHOD: Prepare cake as in hearth method. Place pie plate in preheated 375° oven and bake about 30 minutes until well done.

Finish cake as in hearth method.

DELICIOUS SPONGE CAKE

Versatile sponge cake, although delicious when served plain, is also used in this book in the making of Tipsy Parson Trifle and Banana Pudding.

6 eggs
1 1/4 cups flour
1 1/4 cups sugar
1/2 teaspoon cream of tartar
1/8 teaspoon salt
Juice of 1/2 lemon

Add salt to egg whites and beat until foamy. Add cream of tartar and continue to beat until stiff; add sugar gradually as you beat. Continue to beat until whites hold their shape. Now beat the yellows until light and creamy; add lemon juice, then add whites and beat all together. Carefully fold the flour into the mixture, a little bit at a time. Pour into an ungreased pan.

HEARTH METHOD: Place cake on trivet in preheated Dutch oven. Set oven on pile of coals on hearth, cover and pile coals on the lid. The cake should bake for about 50 minutes; test for doneness. Remove pan from oven; invert and let stand until cold.

MODERN METHOD: Place cake in preheated 300° oven and bake for about 50 minutes or until done. Remove from oven; invert and let stand until cold.

TIPSY PARSON TRIFLE

Although composed of easily available ingredients, when the dish is presented it is considered a very elegant dessert. It is always arranged in the most attractive of bowls. Whether or not it contains enough sherry to cause one to become tipsy is debatable, but it is delicious.

8 cups sponge cake cubes (page 118)
1/2 cup raspberry jam
1 cup sherry
2 eggs
1 egg yolk
1 3/4 cups milk
1/4 cup granulated sugar
1 egg white
1 tablespoon powdered sugar
1 cup heavy cream
1/4 teaspoon vanilla
1/4 cup slivered almonds

Cover one side of the cake cubes with jam. Place half of the cubes, jam side up, in bottom of large clear glass bowl. Moisten with some of the sherry. Top with remaining cake cubes. Add enough additional sherry to moisten cake well.

In saucepan, beat eggs and the egg yolk. Stir in milk and granulated sugar.

HEARTH METHOD: Place the saucepan on trivet over coals. Cook and stir until custard coats a metal spoon. Remove saucepan from heat and place in cool water; stir occasionally.

TO FINISH TRIFLE: Spoon custard over cake.

Beat the egg white to soft peaks. Gradually add powdered sugar, beating until stiff peaks form.

Whip cream with vanilla. Fold into egg whites. Pile mixture atop custard. Set in cool place for several hours or overnight. Garnish with slivered almonds.

MODERN METHOD: Place the saucepan over medium heat. Cook and stir until custard coats a metal spoon. Remove saucepan from heat and place in ice water. Stir occasionally.

Finish trifle as in hearth method.

ROSE GERANIUM CAKE

This is a lovely cake which will fill your kitchen with the aroma of the popular herb Pelargonium graveolens, rose geranium.

1 tablespoon butter
1/4 cup sugar
rose geranium leaves
1/2 cup butter
1 cup sugar
1 egg
2 cups flour
3 teaspoons baking powder
1/2 teaspoon salt
3/4 cup milk
1 teaspoon vanilla

TO PREPARE PAN: With the 1 tablespoon butter generously butter the cake pan. Sprinkle with the 1/4 cup sugar. Arrange the geranium leaves in a pleasing design. Set pan aside.

Cream butter, add sugar, and beat until light and fluffy. Stir in the egg. Sift the dry ingredients together and add alternately with milk and vanilla. Turn into prepared pan.

HEARTH METHOD: Place the plan in preheated Dutch oven. Set oven on pile of coals and put coals on lid. Bake for about 20-25 minutes until the cake tests done. Cool in pan for 10 minutes.

MODERN METHOD: Place pan in preheated 350° oven and bake about 20-25 minutes until cake tests done.

PLAIN PASTRY

Makes two pie crusts; for one crust, half recipe.

2 cups flour
1 teaspoon salt
2/3 cup lard
4 tablespoons cold water

Measure flour and sift with salt. Add lard and cut into flour using two knives. Add water gradually, lightly mixing with fork. Chill for at least 30 minutes. Roll pastry to desired thickness.

LEMON BUTTERMILK CUSTARD PIE

1/2 cup butter
1/2 cup sugar
3 tablespoons flour
4 eggs, beaten
1 cup buttermilk
juice and grated rind of one lemon
dash nutmeg, freshly grated
1/4 teaspoon salt

1 unbaked pie shell (page 122)

Cream butter and sugar; add flour and eggs. Beat until fluffy. Stir in remaining ingredients. Pour into pie shell.

HEARTH METHOD: Place pie on trivet in preheated Dutch oven. Set oven on coals and pile coals on lid. Bake about 30-40 minutes until pie is set.

MODERN METHOD: Bake pie in preheated 350°F oven for 45-50 minutes.

BAKING HINT: If a pie filling is "runny" before baking, it is helpful to arrange the pastry filled pie pan on the trivet in the Dutch oven and then add the filling.

CHESS PIE

This is a traditional Southern pie. It is always made with a bit of white cornmeal.

1/4 pound butter, room temperature
2 cups sugar
1/4 teaspoon salt
1 tablespoon flour
1 tablespoon white cornmeal
4 well-beaten egg yolks
1 cup milk
1 tablespoon vanilla
1 unbaked pie shell (page 122)

Cream butter, sugar, and salt. Add flour and cornmeal and mix well. Stir in the beaten egg yolks and then the milk and vanilla, mixing well. Pour into unbaked pie shell.

HEARTH METHOD: Place pie pan on trivet in preheated Dutch oven. Set oven on coals and pile coals on top. Bake about one hour until the pie is firm in the middle.

MODERN METHOD: Bake pie in preheated 350° oven for about one hour or until firm in the middle.

SUMMER FRUIT COBBLER

A cobbler is a type of deep-dish fruit pie. A true cobbler must have a bottom crust. The pan is lined with thinly rolled pastry and topped with a thicker crust. Use the fruit of your choice; my favorite is peach!

1/2 cup sugar
1 1/2 tablespoons corn starch
freshly grated nutmeg
1/2 teaspoon salt
4 cups ripe fruit, sliced
1/2 cup water
4 tablespoons butter

Pastry for two-crust pie

Roll out half the pastry thinly and line baking dish.

Mix sugar, corn starch, nutmeg, and salt. Stir fruit in this mixture and turn into the pastry-lined dish. Pour in the water and dot with butter.

Roll out the remaining pastry and cover dish (or cut pastry into strips and form lattice on top). Trim and seal edges; slash top to allow steam to escape.

HEARTH METHOD: Set baking dish in preheated Dutch oven, set oven on coal on hearth, and pile coals on lid. Bake for about 45 minutes or until done and brown.

MODERN METHOD: Bake the pie in preheated 350° oven for about 45 minutes or until done.

Serve the cobbler with heavy cream!

FRIED FRUIT PIES

A fried pie was the treat which mothers often put into lard bucket lunch pails for their school children. Apples or peaches are the fruit of choice for these delicious pies.

CRUST

2 cups flour
1/2 teaspoon salt
1 teaspoon baking soda
1/2 cup lard
cold water

Combine flour, salt, and baking soda together in mixing bowl. Using two knives, cut lard into the dry mixture. Sprinkle water over the flour mixture by tablespoons; mix lightly with fork, until enough has been added so that the dough can be shaped into a ball. Allow to set for a while in a cool place. Roll out and cut into rounds using a saucer to measure size. Place 2-3 tablespoons of fruit filling in the center of each round. Wet the edge of the round with cool water, fold over, and press with a fork to seal.

HEARTH METHOD: Heat fat in spider over coals on hearth. Fry the pies in the hot fat until golden brown, turning once. Remove with a slotted spoon. Sprinkle with sugar.

MODERN METHOD: Follow the hearth method, frying the pies in skillet over high heat.

FRUIT FILLING

Fruit: apples, peaches
sugar
spices: nutmeg (freshly grated), cinnamon, allspice

HEARTH METHOD: Cook fruit until thick in small pan set on trivet over coals on hearth. Add sugar and spices to taste.

MODERN METHOD: Prepare as in hearth method, cooking fruit over low heat.

DOUBLE CRUST LEMON PIE

This pie is also referred to as Shaker pie. The slices of lemon in the filling are intriguing.

Pastry for double-crust pie (page 122)

2 lemons
1 1/4 cups sugar
4 eggs, well beaten

Line a pie plate with pastry and set aside. Cut the lemons into very thin slices; remove seeds. In a bowl, mix the lemon slices and sugar. Add the beaten eggs, mix well, pour into pastry. Roll out and adjust top crust, cut slits for the steam to escape. Seal and flute the edges.

HEARTH METHOD: Place pie on trivet in preheated Dutch oven. Set oven on coals on hearth; pile coals on lid. Bake about 35-40 minutes or until done and brown.

MODERN METHOD: Place pie in preheated 400° oven and bake about 35-40 minutes or until done.

MOLASSES CUSTARD PIE

Sorghum molasses was often used as the sweetener in early settlers' pies.

1 cup molasses
1/2 cup buttermilk
1 cup sugar
1/2 teaspoon baking soda
2 tablespoons flour
1/2 teaspoon cinnamon
1/4 teaspoon allspice
1/4 teaspoon ground cloves
3 eggs, beaten

Mix all ingredients together, adding beaten eggs last.

HEARTH METHOD: Put mixture in saucepan and set on trivet placed in preheated Dutch oven. Set oven on coals on hearth and put coals on lid. Bake for about 30 minutes or until firm and done.

MODERN METHOD: Follow hearth directions baking pie in 350° preheated oven. Bake for about 30-35 minutes or until the center of the pie is firm and done.

SWEET POTATO PIE

This recipe contains no spices but relies on lemon to bring out the good flavor.

1 3/4 cups mashed sweet potatoes (about 3 med. potatoes)
1 1/2 cups scalded milk
1 tablespoon butter, melted
1 teaspoon salt
2 large eggs
1 cup sugar
1 teaspoon vanilla extract
1 tablespoon lemon juice

Pastry for one-crust pie

HEARTH METHOD: Place potatoes in pot and cover with water. Hang pot from spit over brisk fire and cook until the potatoes can be pierced with a fork. Remove pot from spit; drain the potatoes and let cool until they can be peeled. Mash the potatoes.

Scald the milk in pan placed on trivet over coals. Do not boil.

Melt butter in small pan placed on trivet over coals.

Mix potatoes, salt, milk, eggs, sugar, butter, vanilla extract, and lemon juice. Pour filling into unbaked pie crust.

Place pie in preheated Dutch oven and set oven over coals on hearth. Put coals on top. Bake about 45 minutes or until a knife inserted in center of pie comes out clean.

MODERN METHOD: Follow hearth method of preparation, scalding milk in pan set over medium heat. Melt butter in small pan over low heat. Bake in 400° oven. Test as in hearth method.

RAISIN PIE

The availability of raisins made this pie especially popular in winter when there was no fresh fruit.

2 cup raisins, seeded
1 1/2 cups boiling water
1/2 cup sugar
3 tablespoons corn starch
1/2 teaspoon salt
rind and juice of one lemon
pastry for two-crust pie

HEARTH METHOD: In a saucepan, combine raisins and water. Place pan on trivet over coals on hearth and boil for 5 minutes. Blend sugar, corn starch, and salt. Add to raisins and cook, stirring until clear. Remove from heat, stir in rind and lemon juice. Cool slightly. Turn into pastry-lined pie plate. Cover with lattice strips.

Place pan in preheated Dutch oven. Set oven on coals on hearth and pile coals on top. Bake about 30 minutes or until golden brown.

MODERN METHOD: Combine raisins and water in saucepan, set over medium heat and boil for 5 minutes. Blend sugar, corn starch, and salt. Add to raisins and cook, stirring until clear. Remove from heat; stir in rind and lemon juice. Cool slightly. Pour into pastry-lined pan. Cover with lattice strips.

Place pan in preheated 425° oven and bake about 30 minutes or until golden brown.

SPRINGTIME STRAWBERRY-RHUBARB PIE

The vegetable rhubarb, Rheum rhaponticum, is also called pieplant. Only the fleshy leafstalks of rhubarb are eaten; in fact the leaves are poisonous. Spring is the time to gather the lovely red stalks and as that is the time for the strawberry harvest; the two can be combined to produce this unforgettable Springtime Strawberry-Rhubarb Pie.

2 cups strawberries
1 1/2 cups sugar
3 cups diced rhubarb
1 tablespoon butter
pastry for two-crust pie (page 122)
3 egg yolks
1/2 cup flour
3 tablespoons milk
3/4 teaspoon nutmeg, freshly grated

Mix strawberries with 1/2 cup sugar, mashing slightly to extract juice. Arrange rhubarb in pastry and dot with butter. Drain extracted juice from strawberries and mix with remaining sugar, egg yolks, flour, milk, and nutmeg. Lay strawberries over rhubarb, then pour mixture over berries. Cover with the pastry. Press edges together to seal; slit top to allow steam to escape.

HEARTH METHOD: Place pie plate in preheated Dutch oven. Set oven over coals and pile coals on top. Bake about 30 minutes or until done and brown.

MODERN METHOD: Place pie in preheated 400°F oven and bake about 30 minutes or until done and brown.

While still hot, sprinkle the pie with sugar.

BUTTERNUT SQUASH PIE

The winter varieties of squash, such as butternut, can be stored many months if kept dry and well above freezing. This meant that the early Americans could enjoy wonderful pies long after the harvest had been completed. Butternut squash makes an especially fine pie.

2 cups baked squash (1 large butternut squash about 1 pound)
2 tablespoons butter
1 cup milk
1/2 cup heavy cream
1/4 cup brown sugar
1/2 cup white sugar
1/2 teaspoon salt
1 teaspoon cinnamon
1/2 teaspoon powdered ginger
1/2 teaspoon nutmeg, freshly grated
1/2 teaspoon ground cloves
2 eggs, beaten
Pastry for one-crust pie (page 122)

TO BAKE SQUASH:

HEARTH METHOD: Cut the squash in half lengthwise and remove the seeds. Lay squash cut side down in pie plate. Put the squash in preheated Dutch oven; set oven on coals on hearth and pile coals on top. Bake for about one hour or until you can easily remove peel.

MODERN METHOD: Prepare squash as in hearth method, baking in preheated 350° oven for about one hour or until it can be easily peeled.

Prepare the filling by mixing 2 cups of the baked squash, butter, milk, cream, sugar (brown and white), salt, and spices. Stir in the beaten eggs; mix well. Put filling mixture in unbaked pie crust.

HEARTH METHOD: Set filled pastry in preheated Dutch oven. Place the oven on coals on hearth and put coals on top. Bake for about 45-50 minutes or until a knife inserted in the middle comes out clean.

MODERN METHOD: Follow hearth method baking pie in 350°F preheated oven for about 30-40 minutes or until it tests done.

VINEGAR PIE

Perhaps frontier women used vinegar as a substitute for lemons, which were hard to obtain. I use my homemade lemon thyme vinegar very effectively in this recipe.

1/4 cup butter
1 1/4 cups sugar
2 tablespoons vinegar
3 beaten eggs
1 teaspoon vanilla
1/3 cup currants
1/2 cup pecans, chopped

Cream together the butter and sugar until light and fluffy. Add the vinegar, eggs, and vanilla and beat well. Sprinkle currants and pecans evenly in pie crust. Pour in the filling mixture.

HEARTH METHOD: Place pie in preheated Dutch oven. Set the oven on pile of coals on hearth. Pile coals on top. Bake for about 45 minutes or until a knife blade inserted in the center comes out clean.

MODERN METHOD: Bake the pie in a preheated 350° oven for about 45 minutes or until pie tests done.

BANANA PUDDING WITH SPONGE CAKE

Did someone discover banana pudding before the invention of vanilla wafers? If not, they should have because it is great made with old-fashioned sponge cake (page 118).

1 cup sugar
2 tablespoons flour
1/4 teaspoon salt
2 cups milk
3 egg yolks
1 teaspoon vanilla extract

1 sponge cake
6 bananas
3 egg whites

TO PREPARE CUSTARD:

HEARTH METHOD: Mix together 3/4 cup sugar and the flour and salt in saucepan. Add milk and mix well. Put the saucepan over boiling water in pan set on trivet over coals on the hearth. Cook until mixture thickens, stirring constantly. Continue cooking the mixture for about 15 minutes, stirring occasionally. Beat the egg yolks. Add a little of the hot mixture to yolks and then add all to mixture. Cook for another 5 minutes. Remove from boiling water and stir in the vanilla extract.

MODERN METHOD: Prepare as in hearth method, cooking mixture in top of double boiler placed over moderate heat.

TO COMPOSE PUDDING:

Line the bottom of an ovenproof dish with slices of sponge cake. Top with a layer of sliced bananas. Cover bananas with some of the custard mixture. Continue layers of cake, bananas, and custard, ending with a layer of custard.

Beat the egg whites until they hold a peak. Add the remaining 1/4 cup sugar and beat until sugar is incorporated and whites are stiff but not dry. Pile the egg whites on top of pudding, being sure that the egg white touches the edge of the dish all the way around.

BANANA PUDDING

HEARTH METHOD: Brown the meringue by passing a heated salamander* above the pudding until browned.

A second method for browning the egg whites is to place the pudding dish in a preheated Dutch oven piling coals on the top only. Allow about 5-10 minutes for browning.

MODERN METHOD: Place pudding dish in preheated 425° oven for about 5 minutes or until nicely browned.

* A salamander is a culinary instrument used for browning pastry. It is made of iron and is long-handled. The salamander was heated in the coals at the hearth and then passed over the pastry, the heat causing it to brown.

BREAD PUDDING

This pudding is especially good when made with homemade bread.

2 cups diced stale bread
4 cups milk
3 eggs, beaten
1/2 cup sugar
1/4 cup butter, melted
1/2 teaspoon salt
1 teaspoon vanilla extract
nutmeg, freshly grated

Soak the diced bread in the milk for about 5 minutes. Add all of the other ingredients to the bread mixture and mix well. Pour the mixture into a greased baking dish.

HEARTH METHOD: Place trivet in heated Dutch oven. Set pudding on trivet and add warm water to come about half way up side of the baking dish. Set the oven on coals on hearth and pile coals on oven lid. Bake the pudding for about one hour, checking that water level is maintained.

MODERN METHOD: Set the pudding dish in a pan; add warm water to come about half way up the side of the pudding dish. Bake in preheated 325° oven for about one hour.

CHRISTMAS PLUM PUDDING

We have made this pudding many times at our Cooking Workshops and it has never disappointed us. Be sure to make the pudding several weeks before you plan to serve it. Store in covered container and sprinkle with brandy from time to time!

(amount for one quart mold)

3/4 cup sifted flour
1/2 teaspoon baking soda
1/2 teaspoon salt
1/2 teaspoon cinnamon
1/4 teaspoon nutmeg,
  freshly grated
1/4 teaspoon ground cloves
1/8 teaspoon ginger
1/3 cup brown sugar

3/4 cups bread crumbs
1/2 cup chopped nutmeats
1/2 cup shredded suet
1/2 cup candied fruit
1 cup seedless raisins
2 eggs, lightly beaten
1/4 cup molasses
3/8 cup milk
1/4 cup brandy

Into a mixing bowl, sift together the flour, soda, salt, cinnamon, nutmeg, cloves, and ginger. Combine this mixture with the brown sugar, crumbs, nuts, suet, fruit, and raisins. Blend in the eggs, molasses, milk, and brandy. Pour the mixture into a buttered mold and cover tightly. Place the mold on a rack over about 2 inches of boiling water in a kettle.

HEARTH METHOD: Cover the kettle and hang above a low fire to steam for about two hours or until the pudding is resistant to slight pressure. Replace boiling water as necessary.

MODERN METHOD: Cover the kettle and place over low heat to steam for about two hours or until it tests done.

Cool pudding in mold for about 10 minutes before removing. Serve with hard sauce (recipe page 152).

CLOTH PUDDING

I was absolutely amazed the first time I saw this type of pudding being made. I could not imagine how one kept the pudding from seeping out. The trick is in the preparation of the pudding cloth which is wrung out in hot water and then sprinkled with flour.

1 1/2 cups flour
2 cups dry breadcrumbs (homemade are best)
1 cup suet, finely chopped
1 1/2 cups currants
1/2 cup sugar
1 teaspoon cinnamon
1/4 teaspoon nutmeg, freshly ground
1 teaspoon baking soda
1 egg, beaten
1 1/2 cups buttermilk

Mix flour, breadcrumbs, suet, currants, sugar, spices, and soda together. Add the egg and buttermilk to the first mixture, mixing to a soft dough. Arrange the prepared pudding cloth in a bowl and spoon the pudding mixture into it. Tie cloth at top but be sure to leave enough room as the pudding will expand. Place the pudding on a rack in a large kettle and add boiling water to cover pudding.

HEARTH METHOD: Hang the kettle over fire and allow to boil 2-21/2 hours. Replace water as needed.

MODERN METHOD: Set the kettle over fire and boil for 2-21/2 hours.

Serve the pudding hot with lemon sauce (recipe page 151).

PERSIMMON PUDDING

This autumn treat is prepared after the first big frost of the season when persimmons are at their finest.

1 1/2 cups persimmon pulp
1 1/2 cups buttermilk
1/2 teaspoon baking soda
1 1/2 cups sugar

1 1/4 cups flour
1/4 teaspoon salt
1/4 teaspoon allspice

Combine all ingredients. Pour into greased ovenproof dish.

HEARTH METHOD: Place dish on trivet in preheated Dutch oven. Pile coals on top. Bake for 20-25 minutes or until center of pudding is firm.

MODERN METHOD: Bake in preheated 350° oven for about 20-25 minutes or until pudding tests done.

Serve pudding warm with whipped cream.

INDIAN PUDDING

Soon after the colonists were introduced to maize (corn), they came to depend on it as a vital staple, sometimes eating it three times a day. Indian pudding was the first truly American dessert. Whereas the Indians had sweetened their concoction with the cooked sap of the maple trees, the colonists were soon using molasses from the West Indies and were adding imported spices.

3 cups milk
1/2 cup molasses
1/2 cup cornmeal
1/2 teaspoon ground ginger
1/2 teaspoon ground cinnamon
1/4 teaspoon salt
2 tablespoons butter

HEARTH METHOD: In saucepan, mix milk and molasses; stir in cornmeal, spices, and salt. Set pan on trivet over coals on hearth. Cook and stir until thick, about 10 minutes. Stir in butter. Turn into a greased ovenproof dish. Set dish on trivet in preheated Dutch oven. Set oven over coals on hearth and pile coals on top. Bake for about one hour until firm and nicely brown.

MODERN METHOD: In saucepan, mix milk and molasses; stir in cornmeal, spices, and salt. Cook over medium heat, stirring until thick, about 10 minutes. Stir in butter. Turn into a greased ovenproof dish. Bake in 300°F oven for one hour or until done.

PUMPKIN PUDDING

Serve this lovely, delicious pudding as a fitting dessert for a traditional Thanksgiving dinner.

1 1/2 cup flour	1 1/2 cup cooked pumpkin
2 teaspoons baking soda	1/4 cup heavy cream
1 1/2 teaspoons cinnamon	1 tablespoon lemon juice
1 teaspoon ground cloves	1/4 cup butter
1/2 teaspoon ground ginger	1 cup brown sugar
pinch salt	3 eggs, beaten

Sift the dry ingredients together. In a second bowl, mix the cooked pumpkin, cream, and lemon juice.

Combine the butter and sugar and beat until fluffy. Add the eggs and beat well. Continue beating for several minutes.

Fold in flour mixture. Spoon the batter into the buttered pudding mold. Cover the mold tightly and set on rack in large kettle. Add enough boiling water to come half way up the side of the mold. Cover the kettle.

HEARTH METHOD: Hang kettle over low fire. Let simmer for about 1 1/2 hours or until pudding is firm in center.

MODERN METHOD: Set kettle over low fire and simmer for about 1 1/2 hours or until done.

Remove mold from kettle; let rest for about 10 minutes, then unmold. Serve warm with whipped cream sprinkled with ginger.

BOTTOM-OF-THE-BARREL APPLE CRISP

This is another recipe that was developed for a museum hearth cooking workshop. The name reveals the status of the apple supply.

apples - 2 or more left in the bottom of the barrel
1/2 cup sugar
2 tablespoons flour
1/2 teaspoon salt
1 teaspoon cinnamon
2 tablespoons butter
1/2 teaspoon freshly rubbed sage or
1 tablespoon fresh sage, chopped

Peel and coarsely slice apples. Arrange layer of apples in baking dish. Mix the dry ingredients and sprinkle half over the apple layer, dot with butter, and sprinkle with sage.

Layer the remainder of apples, then sprinkle with remaining dry ingredients. Sprinkle extra sugar over the top.

HEARTH METHOD: Place baking dish on trivet in prepared Dutch oven; set oven on coals on hearth and pile coals on lid. Bake for about 30 minutes or until the apple are soft and the top is crispy and brown.

MODERN METHOD: Place the baking dish in preheated 350°F oven. Bake for about 30 minutes.

GRANDMAW'S TEA CAKES

No one could ever hope to make tea cakes like my Grandmaw Pagan-Love, but we can try! We never visited Grandmaw but that she offered us one of the delicious treats which she stored in a lard pail. This recipe is as near as I have been able to duplicate hers.

2 cups granulated sugar
1/2 cup butter
1/2 cup lard
3 eggs, beaten
3 cups flour
1/2 teaspoon salt
2 teaspoons baking powder
1/2 teaspoon baking soda
1/2 cup buttermilk
1 teaspoon vanilla

Cream sugar, butter, and lard until light and fluffy.

Add the eggs. Mix one cup of the flour, salt, baking powder, and soda; add to the sugar mixture. Stir in the buttermilk and vanilla, then add more flour, enough to form a soft dough.

Turn the dough onto a floured board and knead until smooth. Roll the dough out to 1/2" thickness and cut in desired shapes.

HEARTH METHOD: Place cakes in lightly greased pan, being sure that they do not touch. Place pan in preheated Dutch oven. Set oven over coals on hearth; put coals on top. Bake for 10-12 minutes or until done. Do not overcook.

MODERN METHOD: Place cakes on lightly greased cookie sheet. Bake in 350° oven for about 10-12 minutes or until done.

MARYLAND ROCKS

Rocks are the best-known of any old Maryland cookie. Make ahead and store to bring out the true flavor.

1 cup butter
1 1/2 cups brown sugar
3 eggs, beaten
1 tablespoon cinnamon
1/2 teaspoon baking soda
21/2 cups flour
1 pound chopped nuts
1 pound raisins
1 pound chopped citron

Cream butter and sugar, add well beaten eggs, and mix well. Sift the dry ingredients together. Use some of the dry mixture to coat the nuts, raisins, and chopped citron. Combine the sugar and egg mixture with the dry ingredients. Mix together thoroughly. Stir in the floured nuts, raisins, and citron.

HEARTH METHOD: Drop by teaspoonfuls on lightly greased pan. Place pan in preheated Dutch oven. Set oven on pile of coals on hearth and put coals on the lid. Bake cookies for about 15 minutes or until done. Do not overbake.

MODERN METHOD: Drop by teaspoonfuls on lightly greased cookie sheet. Bake in preheated 350°F oven for about 15 minutes.

Makes about three dozen cookies.

Part Six:
Sauces and Herbs

SAUCES

Mrs. Beeton, in her *Book of Household Management*, originally published in 1859, says, "Neither poultry, butcher's meat, nor roast game were eaten dry in the middle ages, any more than fried fish is now." The book contains dozens of recipes for sauces: sauce for fish, for geese, for pork, for pudding, for mutton, turkey, poultry, vegetables, wildfowl, tarts, and venison. This is her recipe for sauce "to serve with Hot or Cold Roast Beef."

INGREDIENTS: 1 tablespoon of scraped horseradish, 1 teaspoonful of made mustard, 1 teaspoon of pounded sugar, 4 tablespoonfuls of vinegar.

MODE: Grate or scrape the horseradish very fine, and mix it with the other ingredients, which must be all well blended together; serve in a tureen. With cold meat, this sauce is a very good substitute for pickles.

In Mrs. Beeton's time, sugar was "pinched" from the loaf then worked with mortar and pestle until similar to granulated sugar.

"Made mustard" is prepared mustard. The crushed mustard seeds are mixed with vinegar and other seasonings.

MINT SAUCE

This very simple sauce has long been popular for serving with roast lamb. Mint is one of the most common herbs in our herb gardens and one of the easiest to grow.

1/2 cup fresh mint leaves, chopped
2 tablespoons sugar
1 cup cider vinegar

Gather young mint from the garden and wash to remove grit. Pick the leaves from the stalks and mince them very fine. Put the leaves in a glass bowl. Add sugar and vinegar and stir until the sugar has dissolved. This sauce should be made several hours before it is to be served.

LEMON SAUCE

Be sure to try this sauce served hot on sponge cake!

Butter, size of large egg
1 cup sugar
1 egg, beaten
1/2 teaspoon nutmeg, freshly grated
1 lemon (juice and rind, grated)
1/3 cup boiling water

Cream the butter and sugar well. Add the egg, nutmeg, and juice and rind of lemon. Beat several minutes. Put in saucepan.

HEARTH METHOD: Slowly add boiling water. Set saucepan on trivet placed over coals on hearth. Bring sauce just to boil, stirring constantly, but do not boil.

MODERN METHOD: Prepare sauce as for hearth method. Add boiling water. Bring sauce just to boil over low heat. Do not boil.

HARD SAUCE

This sauce, often served with plum pudding, is either poured over the pudding or served in a dish alongside. It is a rich, simple and delicious sauce.

3/4 cup soft butter
1 1/2 cups sugar
dash of salt
brandy to taste

Cream the butter and gradually beat in the sugar and salt until creamy and quite light. Add brandy to taste; continue beating until thoroughly blended.

VANILLA SAUCE

1/2 cup sugar
1 teaspoon cornstarch
1 cup milk
1/2 cup heavy cream
1 egg yolk, beaten
1 tablespoon butter
1 teaspoon vanilla

Combine sugar and cornstarch in saucepan. Slowly add small amount of the milk and stir until smooth. Add remainder of milk and the cream, stirring until well mixed.

HEARTH METHOD: Set the saucepan on trivet placed over coals on hearth. Cook, stirring, until the mixture begins to thicken. Remove from heat. Stir a small amount of the hot mixture into the beaten egg yolk. Stir the egg mixture into the hot sauce mixture; return to the coals and cook, stirring, for an additional few minutes. Again remove from coals; add butter and vanilla. Stir and set aside to cool.

MODERN METHOD: Follow the hearth method, cooking the mixture over low heat.

Serve this sauce hot with bread pudding or cloth pudding.

PEPPER SAUCE

In the South, all greens such as collards, mustards, and turnips and most fresh and dried peas and beans are served with pepper sauce. The pepper sauce container, usually a cruet, is placed on the table along with the other condiments.

hot peppers, enough to fill chosen container
vinegar, amount required to fill the container

Peppers of any shape or size, the hotter the better, are placed in container. Vinegar is then added to fill the container. Cover and set aside for about a week, at which time it can be tested to see if it has reached desired intensity.

Be sure to add several pepper plants to the other herbs in your garden. The addition of pepper improves the flavor of many vegetables.

HERBS

You will find that many of the recipes in this book contain herbs. Since herbs are such an integral part of early American cooking, those recipes are not listed separately. However, you will find recipes for herbal vinegar, butter and tea on the following pages.

I have grown herbs for several years and enjoy using them in many different ways, but I receive the most satisfaction from my use of the culinary herbs. I enjoy picking herbs from my garden when I begin to prepare a meal. At the museum, I gather needed herbs from the lovely little garden which my herb club, The Friendly Thyme Herb Club, tends.

The purpose of our club is to gain and share knowledge of the growing of herbs. The garden, along with the annual Herb Day which we hold at the museum each June, enables us to reach and share with many others who are interested, or who would like to become interested, in herbs.

Cooking with herbs is fun and exciting. It is best to use fresh herbs, but dried ones will add flavor. Always use twice the amount of fresh herbs as that required of dried herbs.

Add herbs to stews, soups, and sauces during the last 15 minutes of cooking time as the flavor of herbs will quickly dissipate.

Consider growing herbs among your vegetables or flowers or in pots on the porch or patio. You will find that they add flavor, interest, and variety to your meals.

HERBS USED IN COOKING

This is a list of the most common culinary herbs and some of the foods in which I like to use them.

BASIL - Especially good with "summer" vegetables such as squash, tomatoes, onions, and eggplant

CHIVES - Potato soup, squash, biscuits, dumplings, and butter

MARJORAM - Stuffings, stews, beans, and eggs

MINT - Split pea soup, lamb, carrots, and peas

 PARSLEY - Fish, stew, beets, potatoes, chicken, and eggs

ROSEMARY - Chicken, lamb, beef, bread, and fruit

SAGE - Chicken, dressing, bread, pork, eggs, and butter

SUMMER SAVORY - Bean soup, rabbit, fowl, stuffing, cabbage, and pork

TARRAGON - Shrimp, pork, mayonnaise, chicken, beets, fish, andbeans

THYME - Clam chowder, fowl, fish, stew, tomatoes, beans, and onions

HERBAL BUTTER

As soon as the herbs are dried by the morning sun, they should be picked for the butter.

Add about two teaspoons of finely minced herbs to 1/2 cup of softened, unsalted butter. Add 1/2 teaspoon of freshly squeezed lemon juice, and if necessary, salt to taste. Mix thoroughly.

Shape into roll in a double thickness of waxed paper (or if working in a period kitchen, use a clean, damp cloth) and chill for about one-half hour. Slice in rounds of desired thickness.

It is desirable to serve butter flavored with an herb that complements the dish to be served. Among the herbs which make excellent butter are rosemary, thyme, chives, mint, sage, and tarragon.

HERBAL TEA

Herbal tea requires lots of experimentation in order to find a combination which the drinker finds pleasant and refreshing. Try all the combinations of which you have heard and then begin to add new or different flavors. Some of the herbs commonly used for herbal tea are: mint, lemon balm, lemon verbena, thyme, sage, rose or other scented geraniums, marjoram, rosemary, and bee balm. Honey is the sweetener of choice for herbal tea.

Heat your teapot by adding boiling water and allowing it to set for a few minutes. Pour out the water and then put into the pot a handful (or about 2 tablespoons per cup) of dried herbs (or twice that amount of fresh ones) which have been crushed in the hands. Fill the pot with briskly boiling water. Cover and allow to steep for about 15 minutes. Covering the pot with a tea cozy is charming and helps to keep the pot nice and hot.

HERBAL VINEGAR

Herbal vinegar can be used in salads, for degreasing the roasting pan, for marinades, and as an ingredient in the preparation of many dishes.

Pick the herbs to be used as soon as they are dry from the morning dew.

Fill a glass container half full of herbs which have been slightly crushed with the hands. Completely fill the container with a good grade of vinegar—preferably wine, either red or white. Cover tightly.

Set the container in the herb garden for about two weeks. Strain through cheesecloth into large glass container. Pour into decorative bottles, adding fresh sprigs of the herb as garnish.

Among the herbs which are used for vinegar are basil, tarragon, oregano, salad burnet, mint, sage, chives, and thyme.